Clocks

THE SMITHSONIAN ILLUSTRATED LIBRARY OF ANTIQUES

General Editor: Brenda Gilchrist

Clocks

Douglas H. Shaffer

COOPER-HEWITT MUSEUM

The Smithsonian Institution's National Museum of Design

ENDPAPERS
Drawings of clocks based on designs by Piranesi. Details from
Comment discerner les styles: le style Piranesi, epoque Louis XVI,
Edouard Rouveyre, editor, published in Paris about 1900. Picture
Collection, Cooper-Hewitt Museum Library

FRONTISPIECE
The famous girandole design by Lemuel Curtis, called by some
America's most beautiful clock. Not many examples remain today.
The case is gilded wood with brass side arms; the pierced hands
are a distinctive Curtis style. American, Concord, New Hampshire,
1816–21. Henry Francis du Pont Winterthur Museum, Winterthur,
Del.

PLATE I
Inlaid mahogany Hepplewhite-style tall clock. Attached inside
the door is a document from the original owner stating that
Griffith Owen made the clock for him. Daniel Longaker made the
case. American, Pennsylvania, 1802. Private collection

This book is dedicated to my wife, Caroline

Art Director, Design: Joseph B. Del Valle

Text Editor: Joan Hoffman

Picture Editor: Lisa Little

"*Y*ou *dominate our parlor, standing as you do much taller than any of the human occupants of the house. Your dignity is immense and your moods steady—you can quiet me from elation just as you can lift me from melancholy. You are a friend to all of us, a regulator on the speed of our lives, and a faithful link between a generation now gone and a generation yet to come. You keep reminding us of our place in the scheme of all things with a special finger that points to our days and a little harvest moon that travels in our private heaven. You are a spokesman for time as you whisper a gentle cadence for the marching seconds, and ring your bell to mark the passing of each hour's parade. You have the special power to lift past into present, to make that which had lived be alive again. You are the voice of my home—may those who follow me listen too, and through the inward searching you inspire, also learn of peace, of beauty, and of love.*"

This unsigned note, found inside the handsome tall clock (or grandfather clock, as most of us say today) shown in plate 1, is witness to a special affection rarely offered to other types of furniture.

A clock can be, all at once, historically interesting, mechanically intriguing and artistically captivating. It can also, for some of us, awaken a deep emotional response. When that happens, we become collectors. It is to all who are in the early stages of so becoming that this book is directed.

Contents

1 Introduction

By convention, "clock" has come to mean a generally non-portable device for simulating, measuring and displaying the passage of time. Similarly, "watch" has come to mean a generally portable device with the same purpose. Since the word *clock* derives from the Middle Dutch *clocke*, meaning "clock" or "bell," and is related to various other words meaning "bell"—for example, the German *Glocke* and the French *cloche*—some writers insist that a clock, as defined above, must strike at predetermined times; if it doesn't strike, they say, it should be called a timepiece. A further semantic difficulty is sometimes raised over the question of portability. A chronometer, for instance, and a carriage clock (plate 2), which is handled and has its own carrying case, are both small timepieces and obviously portable, yet they are quite as obviously not what we call watches.

Let us resolve all such semantic difficulties by agreeing that in this book "clock" shall mean a mechanical timekeeper that may or may not have some secondary capability, such as a striking action, and that normally operates in a stationary position; while "watch" shall mean a mechanical timekeeper that likewise may or may not have some secondary capability and that normally is carried on the person. Most general remarks about timekeepers will apply to both clocks and watches, but to simplify matters we shall usually refer to clocks alone. Watches are discussed separately in Chapter 5, "Time in a Pocket."

Timekeepers can be designed to show absolute time, so that one may say, "The fire began at twelve minutes past three P.M." They can also be designed to show elapsed time, so that one may say, "The fire burned for one hour and ten minutes before being brought under control." The earliest timekeepers—such as sundials, hourglasses, candle clocks and lamp clocks—were generally adapted to one or the other of these modes of timekeeping, but not to both. Sundials (plates 3–5) relate the sun's position directly to a number on a scale that approxi-

2.
Eight-day carriage clock. This example, made by the Boston Clock Company about 1890, is notable for being American (most carriage clocks of the period were French) and for having the time and strike spring barrels mounted on the same arbor, an unusual arrangement. The case is lacquered brass and glass; the dial, white enamel. Private collection

3

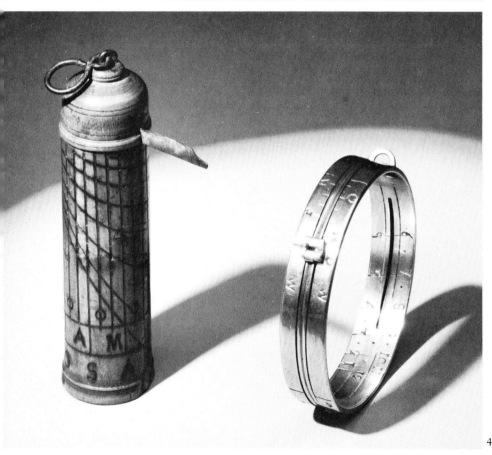

4

3.
Portable sundials with minute wheels. Left: by Claude Dunod, German, Düsseldorf, 1714. Right: by Thomas Wright, English, London, 1726–48. Metropolitan Museum of Art, New York, gift of Mrs. Stephen D. Tucker, 1903

4.
Two portable sundials. Left: cylinder dial, English, c. 1730. Right: ring dial, European, eighteenth–nineteenth century. Metropolitan Museum of Art, New York, gift of Mrs. Stephen D. Tucker, 1903

5.
Paper-faced portable wooden cube sundial with one horizontal dial and four vertical ones. German, Nuremberg, c. 1780–1821. Metropolitan Museum of Art, New York, gift of Mrs. Stephen D. Tucker, 1903

5

mates the hour on a modern clock. (The approximation arises because clocks display mean solar time while sundials display true solar time. The difference over the course of a year can be as much as twenty minutes.) In contrast with the shadow on a sundial, which indicates the hour, the indicators of other timekeepers—the steady burning of a rope, candle or oil supply, or the flow of sand in an hourglass—furnish a measure of elapsed time independent of the time of day.

Clepsydras, or water clocks, are known to have been used in both modes. The simplest clepsydra could measure elapsed time by the interval required for a flow of water to fill or empty out of a container. When the flow of water into and out of the container was maintained at a uniform rate, a more sophisticated clepsydra could show absolute time. There are records of complicated water-controlled timekeepers, as well—for example, we know of a remarkable astronomical water clock built in China in the eleventh century and associated with the name of Su Sung that embodied the concept of cutting time into short intervals and counting them, a principle employed by all mechanical clocks. It also displayed a rotating celestial sphere.

Sundials, sandglasses, clepsydras, candles and the like are, when compared with mechanical clocks, inadequate for the regulation and synchronization of modern human affairs. (It must be admitted that some demands of current technology are not satisfied even by mechanical clocks, but such sophisticated timekeepers as atomic and crystal-oscillator clocks are not within the purview of a book on antique clocks.) The date of the first mechanical clock is not known, nor is the name of its inventor. Evidence suggests that the first mechanical clocks were made shortly before A.D. 1300, but the earliest extant example dates from the late fourteenth century. Until the middle of the seventeenth century mechanical timekeepers were erratic and imprecise. To find that a clock of that period errs by fifteen minutes one day and thirty minutes the next is not unusual. It was the introduction of the *pendulum* in 1657 and of the *hairspring* in about 1675 that led to the evolution of accurate mechanical time-keepers.

Our study of the clock will cover three aspects: history—the clock's development and its reflection of contemporary styles or events; mechanics—the clock's timekeeping mechanism and operating appendages; and artistry—the clock's decorative qualities and workmanship.

We shall also consider functional structure. Every mechanical clock must have a source of energy, for clocks mark the passage of time by allowing energy to dissipate at a controlled rate. There must be a device that governs the rate at which the energy is allowed to dissipate (escape); this device is called an *escapement*. There must be a facility for recording and displaying the rate at which the energy escapes. There may be adjunctive mechanisms that strike bells, play music, operate dancing figures, maintain calendars, sound alarms and so forth. Lastly, there must be a mechanical connection among all the above. These five elements—energy source, escapement, display, adjunctive mechanisms and mechanical connections—will be our basis for describing a clock as an operating device.

The plan of this book is novel. We shall begin with a detailed examination of one particular American clock. Then we shall proceed through American horological history to inspect the ancestors and contemporaries of, and successors to, our basic clock. Thereafter we shall survey the craft of clockmaking in Europe during the Renaissance and in Holland, France, England, Japan and elsewhere from the seventeenth century onward. Finally, we shall deal with watchmaking: first, the European craft, beginning in the sixteenth century, and then the American industry after 1850.

No book of this kind can be comprehensive. Rather, an attempt has been made to achieve a workable balance between breadth and depth, and to do so in a way that will encourage further reading. The coverage of American clocks, though far from complete, is more thorough than that of clocks of any other country. This emphasis is not accidental but a deliberate acknowledgment of the predominant interests of collectors on this side of the Atlantic and of the fact that, over here, American clocks are the ones most often available.

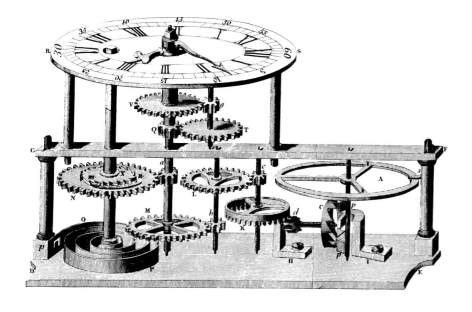

Clock movement showing four of the five elements of a clock's functional structure. The energy source is a coiled spring (O), the escapement is a crown wheel (C) and verge (p-p) with a balance wheel (A), the display is a conventional dial (R-S) and all elements are mechanically connected by gears, as shown. There is no adjunctive mechanism. Illustration from *Treatise on Clock and Watch Making* by Thomas Reid, Edinburgh, 1826

2   Our Basic Clock

Clockmaking can be either a craft or an industry. The first and most important lesson to learn is that there is a difference between the two. Clockmaking was born as a craft and was so practiced for several hundreds of years. Its evolution into an industry was completed within a relatively short time. Once the change was made and the industry established, little further practice of the craft was seen.

Until the first decade of the nineteenth century, all clocks, both in America and in Europe, came from the shops of individual craftsmen. Each clock was an independent project, its parts carefully formed, fitted and finished to produce that one clock—although in shops where craftsmen worked together, there was probably some specialization in the making of the different parts. Many skills were needed to produce a complete clock; joiners, turners, metalworkers and others contributed their talents. But the final product remained crafted handwork.

The industry, on the other hand, was characterized by the manufacture, with specially designed machinery, of interchangeable parts for assembly into complete clocks. The "clockmaker" of the industrial period was removed from the actual product, for he now merely designed a clock or the machinery with which its components were to be manufactured.

The one clock that had the greatest effect in transforming the craft into an industry was the thirty-hour wooden-movement pillar-and-scroll shelf clock developed by Eli Terry of Plymouth, Connecticut, in the second decade of the nineteenth century (plate 6). Its introduction changed the world's clockmaking forever. In America, it generated an industry in southern New England that brought economic health to the region even as the craft itself was fading away elsewhere. The pillar and scroll is a very important clock historically, mechanically, artistically. A close study of it will help in an under-

Colorplate 1.
A standard pillar-and-scroll wooden shelf clock. This example, marketed by H. Dexter of Stockbridge, New York, bears a label proclaiming its Connecticut manufacture and asserting that no better clock can be bought. The wooden movement was made by the prominent clockmaker Mark Leavenworth (1774–1849) of Waterbury, Connecticut; the mahogany-veneered case is the standard Eli Terry pillar-and-scroll design. The tops of the scrolls have been skillfully restored with lighter-colored wood; such repairs are common. (This is the "basic" clock of this chapter—see plates 7–11 for views of the movement.) American, Connecticut, 1820–30. Private collection

standing of the operation of clocks in general and will also provide useful perspectives for an analysis of other clocks.

Let us take for our study the Mark Leavenworth pillar-and-scroll clock shown in colorplate 1, which is typical of the thousands made by Connecticut clockmakers between 1820 and 1830. A clear glass panel in the upper part of the door forms most of the front of the clock. Through the glass can be seen the *dial*, which is the means for showing the passage of time. The dial has two hands, the *minute hand*, which revolves once an hour and indicates minutes within the hour, and the *hour hand*, which revolves once in twelve hours, or twice a day. The minute and hour scales lie on concentric circles within an annulus known as the *chapter ring*. These scales may be indicated by markers or numbers, or both; our pillar and scroll has an hour scale marked 1 through 12 and a minute scale of sixty unnumbered dots. Such a dial-and-hand display is by far the commonest on clocks. It may seem gratuitous to explain all this, but we must remember that different displays are found, especially on earlier clocks, that may not be so easily recognizable.

6.
The clock that revolutionized American clockmaking—Eli Terry's pillar-and-scroll wooden shelf clock. The earliest model featured the escape wheel and pendulum in front of the dial, as here. The case is mahogany veneer. American, Plymouth, Connecticut, 1816. American Clock and Watch Museum, Bristol, Conn.

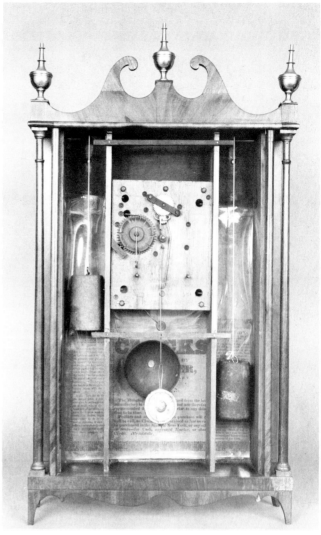

7

8

7.
Clock in colorplate 1 with the door removed, revealing the pendulum, the bell, the label and the full dial.

8.
Clock in colorplate 1 with the dial and hands removed, revealing the movement, weights and entire channel boards. Each weight cord passes over its own pulley (not visible) in the top of the case.

Removing the door of our clock reveals what was previously hidden behind the painted lower section (plate 7). Now visible are a label, an iron bell and a *pendulum*. The label is the printed paper pasted to the backboard of the clockcase. It identifies the maker or seller; gives directions for setting up and operating the clock; frequently makes claims about patents, guarantees and qualities (all of which claims may be suspect); and sometimes offers such almanac-type information as census lists or postal rates. The bell is the round dark object mounted on the backboard; it rings the hours. The smaller, lighter disk is the bob of the pendulum. The function of the pendulum, which is a vital part of the mechanism, will be seen shortly.

For the next stage of disassembly the dial and hands are removed (plate 8). The rectangular object pinned in the upper center of the clock, and previously hidden by the dial, is the *works* of the clock— or, to use the preferred term, the *movement*. Hanging on either side of the movement, and separated from it by the vertical *channel boards*, are the *weights*. The weights provide the driving force, or source of energy. Also visible is the *striking hammer*, directly below the movement and just above the bell. It sounds the hours by hitting the bell.

An oblique view of the movement from the right side (plate 9) allows observation of its gross structure. What can be seen is a series of gears called a *gear train*. The gears have horizontal axles, or *arbors*, held in place between two vertical boards, or *plates*. Each arbor has a steel pin in both its ends; these pins, or *pivots*, fit into holes in the plates and thus the arbors are held in proper position for rotation. The arbor at the bottom—the starting point of the gear train—has a thick section around which the weight cord is wrapped. This thick section is called the *drum*. The heavy wooden posts running between the plates at the top and bottom of the movement are the *pillars*. They position the plates properly with respect to each other and give structural rigidity to the movement.

A close look will show that each arbor, except the one with the drum, carries both a small and a large toothed member. The large member, which may have several dozen teeth, is called a *wheel*. The small member, which typically has six to ten teeth, called *leaves*, is a *pinion*. These wheels and pinions form the gears that make up a gear train. When a gear train operates, power is transmitted from the wheel on one arbor to the pinion on the next, so that successive arbors in the

9.
Clock in colorplate 1: movement seen from the right. The wooden gearing of the time train is now visible.

10.
Clock in colorplate 1: movement seen from the front. The two wheels are the escape wheel (upper center) and the count wheel, which controls the striking sequence. The C-shaped metal verge at the bottom of the escape wheel is clearly visible.

11.
Clock in colorplate 1: movement seen from the left. The wooden gearing of the strike train is now visible.

train rotate at higher and higher speeds. The gear train shown here drives the hands and is called the *time train*, or *going train*.

A frontal view of the movement (plate 10) shows the ends of the pivots that pass through the front plate. Slightly above the center we find two concentric arbors with squared ends that pass through the plate and project well out in front (also see plates 9 and 11 for a clearer view of these projecting arbors). These arbors will have the hands of the clock affixed to them. The inner one carries the minute hand. The pipelike outer one, which is hollow and not quite so long as the minute-hand arbor, carries the hour hand. Hidden behind the front plate is an intermediate *reduction gear* connecting these concentric arbors and effecting a twelve-to-one change in rotational rate so that the minute hand can go twelve times as fast as the hour hand. The gears on the hand arbors together with the reduction gear constitute what is called the *motion work*, or *motion train*.

To the right of the hand arbors can be seen a wire that ends in a loop surrounding the upper part of the pendulum rod. This is the *crutch wire*; it provides the connection between the movement proper and the pendulum. The upper end of the crutch wire is attached to an arbor that carries a roughly C-shaped steel piece, the *verge*. The verge

10

11

is positioned to intersect the travel of the last wheel in the time train. This wheel is called the *escape wheel*. The natural frequency of swing of the pendulum determines the rate at which the escape wheel is allowed to turn. Here the escape wheel turns half a tooth with each tick of the pendulum. The pendulum on this clock requires half a second for a full swing in one direction, so the escape wheel advances one tooth per second.

Two other items to notice on the front plate are the squared steel posts emerging on either side of the pendulum rod near the loop of the crutch wire. These are extensions of the arbors with the weight-cord drums and are used for winding the clock. A key or crank is slipped through a winding hole in the dial onto the end of the arbor and turned in one direction to wind the weight cord onto the drum. The arbor at right is for the time; the one at left is for the strike. The two winding holes can be seen in plate 7.

A side view of the movement from the left (plate 11) shows a second gear train. This one causes the clock to strike on the hour and is called the *strike train*. The clock's two gear trains are separate from each other, and each has a weight as its source of power.

In the center of this side view, directly in back of the front plate of the movement, can be seen a flat object shaped somewhat like a thick razor blade that is mounted on the last arbor of the strike train. This is called the *fan-fly*, or simply *fly*, and it acts to control the speed of the strike train during the striking operation. It is a simple governor and works by presenting a surface for air resistance. A pin fixed on the minute-hand arbor releases a lock on the strike train at each hour and allows the train to run enough to strike one sequence. The striking sequences sound the hours progressively from 1 through 12 and then repeat. Control of the length of the striking sequence is accomplished through the *count wheel* (also called the *locking plate*), which is the irregularly notched wheel mounted outside the front plate near the upper-left corner seen in plate 10. Count-wheel striking, such as we have on this clock, is the simplest of several striking systems. If the hour shown and the hour struck do not agree, the strike train can be tripped manually until the two agree again.

Earlier, we identified five important elements of a clock's functional structure: energy source, escapement, display, adjunctive mechanisms and mechanical connections. Let us now examine our basic clock with respect to these factors, as an example of how this might be done with any clock. To begin with, the energy is supplied by the force of gravity as it acts on the weights to produce tension; the tension gives torque to the drums that drive the time and strike gear trains. This sort of clock is called a weight-driven clock. Secondly, the escapement— that is, control of the energy received from the descending time-train weight—is provided by the pendulum, verge and escape wheel. The exact shape of the verge and its relation to the toothed escape wheel are important; the type used in our clock causes the time train to back up slightly at the end of each pendulum swing. This sort of escapement is known as an *anchor*, or *recoil*, *escapement*. Thirdly, the display of time is, as previously noted, a conventional twelve-hour dial with two hands. Fourthly, there is one adjunctive mechanism, which strikes each hour on a bell. Finally, the mechanical connection is a gear train (the time train) composed of wheels and pinions that receive energy from the descending weight and drive the hands at a rate controlled by the escapement.

As already told, it was Eli Terry who turned clockmaking in America from a craft into an industry and, while so doing, produced the pillar-and-scroll clock. Terry was born in South Windsor, Connecticut, in 1772 and died in 1852. He was apprenticed to Daniel Burnap (1759–1838), who had earlier been apprenticed to the English-born clockmaker Thomas Harland (1735–1807), now often called the father of Connecticut clockmaking.

Terry made clocks in the standard manner during the closing years of the eighteenth century. In 1797 he was granted the first clock-related patent in American history. It was not until 1807, however, that the direction and extent of his innovative approach became apparent. In that year he signed a contract with two businessmen named Porter, from Waterbury, Connecticut, to manufacture four thousand movements for tall clocks, all the movements to be made at his Plymouth, Connecticut, factory within three years. (At this time, incidentally, tall clocks were not called grandfather clocks. That term did not become popular until after 1876, when the song "My Grandfather's Clock" was published by the celebrated American composer Henry Clay Work, best remembered today for his Civil War song "Marching Through Georgia.")

The Terry-Porter contract created quite a stir, even amusement, if only because it was clear that, under prevailing methods of clock manufacture, merely a fraction of that number could be made in the allotted time. Moreover, few believed that the market could absorb anywhere near four thousand tall clocks. But all doubts about the contract proved to be groundless.

Terry fulfilled his end of the bargain by designing and constructing machinery that allowed him to fabricate identical components for the clocks and thus reduce the major problem to one of assembly. This production of clocks with interchangeable parts was the first example of mass production for peaceful purposes in American history. (Interchangeable parts for firearms had been made a decade or so earlier at Eli Whitney's gun factory near New Haven, Connecticut.) The market for clocks, furthermore, proved to be much larger than had been anticipated.

Connecticut clock manufacture, up to 1810, had been almost entirely confined to tall clocks. Eli Terry, sensing that a substantial market awaited modestly priced small clocks for shelf or mantel, began a period of experimentation that would last nearly a decade and eventually enable him to produce an attractive small clock that could sell for as little as fifteen dollars and still return a profit. That clock was the pillar and scroll, which was ready for market by 1818.

The historical importance of this clock, once again, is immense. It pointed the way from clocks laboriously handmade by craftsmen to clocks machine-made in quantity. In so doing, it established an industry that was to become a significant part of the economic life of Connecticut for the next century and a half. It was the first clock deliberately designed to appeal to a mass market.

Mechanically, the pillar-and-scroll clock has two features worth particular notice. First, the movement is largely of wood. Second, it is a weight-driven shelf clock. Earlier Connecticut clockmakers had used wood as a raw material for their less expensive movements, although no one doubted that movements made of brass and steel were more durable. But in the unsettled period between the American Revolution and the War of 1812, brass was a scarce and expensive commodity. Clocks with wooden movements had been made in southern Germany as early as the seventeenth century, but brass was the standard material used in America when available and when customers were prepared to pay the price. Such wooden movements as were used in eighteenth-century Connecticut tall clocks were more nearly variations, in wood, of brass movements than adaptations of the much earlier German models. The wooden movements made by Terry to fulfill the Porter tall-clock contract were constructed after an improved design of his own.

When Terry planned his shelf clock, he again determined to use wood, both because brass was still scarce and because he needed a material from which parts could be easily mass-produced with machinery he could design.

The dial of the pillar and scroll is of painted wood. The plates are of quartersawed oak. The wheels are of cherry, and the pinions and arbors are of laurel. The thin brass escape wheel is the only exception to the general use of wood for the wheels. A metal escape wheel is a standard feature of such wooden-movement clocks.

The fact that the pillar and scroll is a shelf clock driven by weights is also significant. Even though the wooden-movement weight-driven tall clocks of the period required a weight drop of nearly 5 feet (152.4 centimeters) to manage a one-day run, thanks to Terry's redesigned gearing, the pillar and scroll successfully ran a full day with a weight drop of only 16½ inches (41.9 centimeters). Finally, Terry correctly judged that an attractive price would more than offset the fact that his new clock, because it used weights, was too heavy to be easily portable.

The pillar-and-scroll case, as seen in colorplate 1, is essentially a rectangular box. It is 21 inches (53.3 centimeters) high, 13 inches

(33 centimeters) wide and 3 inches (7.6 centimeters) deep, and is embellished with thin, tapered pillars on the sides, a graceful scrolled crest with turned brass finials across the top, and a base with bracket feet and a full skirt across the bottom. The whole is executed in mahogany veneer, by far the most popular wood for clockcases. The split door has a reverse-painted glass pane called the *tablet* in the lower section and a clear glass pane in the upper.

The basic proportions of the clock were under Terry's control only in the sense that he could have made it taller and wider. The minimum width was dictated by the requirements of the movement and the two weight channels; the minimum height, by the requirements of sufficient weight fall to run the clock a full day.

The decorative surround, however, was wholly under Terry's control, and displays many masterful touches. The scrolls of the crest, which normally bend slightly toward the back of the clock, are exquisitely proportioned. The side pillars have a very subtle taper toward the top, a feature likely to go unnoticed until one encounters a low-grade restoration in which the taper has been omitted; then one wonders why the clock appears clumsy. The skirt across the base between the delicate bracket feet complements the scrolls and provides appropriate decorative support. The pleasing proportions of the brass finials at the top in relation to their supporting bases (called *chimneys* or *plinths*) and to the scroll top as a whole are often overlooked until, once again, some inexperienced restorer provides replacements that are too large or too small. The backboard projecting to either side serves as a good background for the pillars, and they in turn help to disguise the fact that the case is narrower in front than in back.

The door, to repeat, is usually provided with two glass panes, the upper of which is clear to allow viewing of the dial, the lower of which is decorative. These decorative panes, the tablets, are painted on the reverse side by using the glass-painting technique in which the highlights are put on before the background. Landscape scenes were the most popular and were usually surrounded with a gold-leaf border. Often the scenes are interrupted by an oval clear spot centered at the rest position of the pendulum. The motion of the brass pendulum bob behind this clear spot adds a dramatic note to the scene portrayed on the tablet.

In short, Terry's pillar-and-scroll clock earns a collector's respect in all three of the aspects we have been considering. It is historically important, for it marked the transition from hand- to mass-production and helped to establish an industry in Connecticut that flourished almost to our own day. It is mechanically important, for its movement, although standard in function, is an innovative design executed in wood. It is artistically important, for its case is beautiful in concept and execution and indeed is considered by many to be among the loveliest in the whole of American clockmaking.

3   Clocks from America

The clockmaking craft was practiced in America for more than a hundred years before Eli Terry's pillar-and-scroll clock became a reality. During these years the skills of the Old World were blended with those of the New to produce increasingly distinctive timepieces. Nearly all American-made clocks of this early period were tall clocks, and most were made for local sale. The two most important clockmaking centers in the colonies were the Middle Atlantic and New England regions. The clocks and clockmakers of both these areas are the focus of this chapter.

Middle Atlantic Clocks   Most of the Middle Atlantic colonies supported the craft of clockmaking—Delaware, New Jersey, New York and Maryland among them. Prominent clockmakers from these centers included the Crow brothers, George, Jr., and Thomas (Delaware), Isaac Pearson (New Jersey), Nathaniel Dominy (New York) and Goldsmith Chandlee (Maryland and Virginia). But by far the largest number of clockmakers worked in Pennsylvania, and for the balance of this section, Pennsylvania clocks and clockmakers will be discussed as representative of the entire Middle Atlantic region.

The premier eighteenth-century Pennsylvania clockmaker was David Rittenhouse (1732–1796). Born near Germantown, he was a Renaissance man whose genius encompassed the fields of astronomy, mathematics and surveying as well as clockmaking. Among other achievements, Rittenhouse served as treasurer of Pennsylvania (1777–89), professor of astronomy at the University of Pennsylvania (1779–82), first director of the United States Mint (1792–95) and successor to Benjamin Franklin as president of the American Philosophical Society (1791–96). One of his most renowned clocks is the astronomical masterpiece now at the Drexel Institute in Philadelphia. Completed in 1774, it is a worthy candidate for honors as the most outstanding *complicated clock* ever built in America.

Colorplate 2.
Engraved sheet-brass dial of the Thomas Harland tall clock shown in plate 24 (see page 38). Noteworthy details include the Four Seasons in the spandrels, the painted moon dial, the global maps, the signature plate, the pierced hands, the seconds dial above the hands and the calendar aperture below them. American, Norwich, Connecticut, c. 1774. Private collection

Pennsylvania was home also to many other outstanding early American horological craftsmen, for William Penn had established a colony in which Quakers and members of other religious groups could live peacefully side by side, a condition rarely achieved in the colonies of New England. To Pennsylvania, then, came not only Penn's fellow Englishmen but also Germans, Scotch-Irish and others. Of particular interest to us are the German and English clockmakers who settled in Philadelphia and vicinity at the beginning of the eighteenth century, flourished at their trade and handed on to apprentices and successors their traditional national styles.

Distinctions between English and German styles appear in both movements and cases. Pennsylvania tall clocks were made in eight-day and thirty-hour varieties, nearly all with a strike train that sounded the hours on a bell. With very rare exceptions, they were constructed with brass plates for the movement, steel arbors and pinions, and brass wheels. The characteristics below apply to "pure" English and German movements, but many blends of the two types can be found.

Thirty-hour, English: Time and strike trains are run by a single weight suspended from a continuous chain; winding is accomplished by pulling up the weight on the strike side. The strike train is to the right of the time train—the reverse of the common arrangement. The pendulum has a *suspension spring*—a flattened upper part of the rod firmly clamped in place and flexible enough to permit the pendulum to swing freely.

Thirty-hour, German: The strike train is to the right of the time train, again the reverse of the common arrangement. Each train, however, is powered by its own weight, and winding is accomplished by pulling on the counterweighted ends of the chains. The pinions are of *lantern* construction. (Leaves of a lantern pinion are individual wires, the pinion resembling a cylindrical cage. *Cut pinions*, on the other hand, are cut from solid stock more in the fashion of a wheel. It is the cut type that is found on the English thirty-hour and on the pillar-and-scroll clock as well, although the latter's pinions are of wood.) The pendulum has a *trapeze suspension*—an arrangement with the pendulum rod hooked over a wire or cord that can swing like a trapeze.

Eight-day, English and German: Both varieties have the conventional configuration of strike train on the left, time on the right. Both are wound by cranks inserted through winding holes in the dial. The principal differences are that the English type has cut pinions, the German lantern pinions, and that the English pendulum has a suspension spring, the German a trapeze suspension.

The case designs of Pennsylvania tall clocks make a fascinating study in themselves. Local styles associated with Philadelphia, Lancaster County and western Pennsylvania evolved. The influence of Chippendale and Hepplewhite was blended with Quaker simplicity or Pennsylvania Dutch folk art in varying proportions. The clocks illustrated here were chosen to display a range from primitive to sophisticated types and from unified to eclectic styles, both German and English.

There are generally three distinct sections to a tall-clock case: the *hood*, or upper part (sometimes called the *bonnet*), which can be lifted to get to the movement; the *waist*, or center part (sometimes called the *trunk*), which contains a door for access to the weights and pendulum; and the *base*, or lower part (sometimes called the *plinth*). The connoisseur will judge the relative proportions of these sections. The most common fault in design is a too-thick waist, which gives the case an appearance best described as clumsy. Sometimes one sees a case in which the base is too short for the waist. It is always possible that such a case was poorly designed, but what is more likely is that a latter-day carpenter shortened the base to accommodate a low ceiling.

Also to be considered in evaluating the design of a case are questions other than those involving proportion. First, regarding the hood: What is the style of fretwork or crest design? Do the finials and finial chimneys blend with the crest in style and size? Are freestanding corner columns or applied half columns used, and if they are, in what manner are they finished? With fluting or stopped fluting? With capitals carved or of brass? Then the waist: What construction details, such as dovetailing, pegging and mitering, are to be observed? Does the door have carving, edge beading or other decorative detail? Lastly, the base: Is there decorative detail on the front panel, perhaps applied carving or inlay work? Are there decorative touches at the corners, such as beveling or fluting? Do the feet agree in style with the case as a whole? This last question is raised because feet were often damaged and are likely to have been replaced with something the replacer regarded as an improvement over the original.

The painted flat-top tall clock by Jacob Godschalk (d. 1781) of Philadelphia shown in colorplate 3 exhibits a simple or primitive case style. The dial, of brass with applied silvered-brass chapter ring, bespeaks the pre-Revolutionary period, while the engraved pattern of the dial center is characteristic of the Schuylkill Valley. The absence of winding holes through the dial identifies it as a thirty-hour tall clock. (Typical American tall clocks that need to be wound every day— or every thirty hours—are wound not by key or crank but by raising the weights. This is accomplished by opening the waist door and pulling on the counterweighted ends of the ropes or chains that hold the weights. This type of winding applies only to thirty-hour tall clocks. Clocks that run a week—or eight days—are wound by inserting a crank through winding holes in the dial and winding the rope cables onto the drums in the movement, as with the pillar-and-scroll clock.)

The clock in plate 1 (see page 5) made by Griffith Owen, Jacob Godschalk's brother-in-law and apprentice, shows a well-developed Hepplewhite style. It has flame-and-urn finials with reeded chimneys,

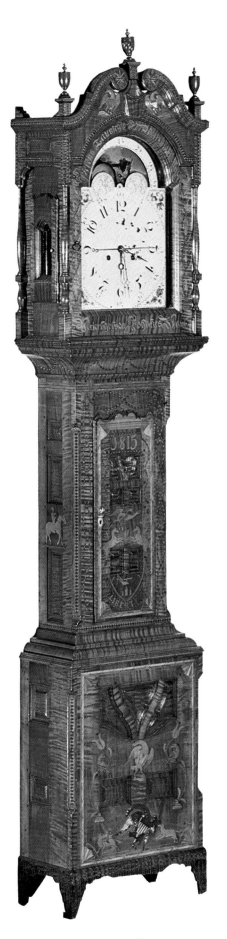

COLORPLATE 3

COLORPLATE 4

Colorplate 3.
Painted tulipwood flat-top tall clock by Jacob Godschalk. The thirty-hour English-type movement has the strike train on the right. The decorative detailing below the cornice of the hood is called dentilwork. American, Philadelphia, c. 1770. Private collection

Colorplate 4.
German-style tall clock, dated 1815, by John Paul, Jr. (1789–1868). Paul made the ornate curly maple and walnut with ivory case as well as the movement. American, Elizabethville, Pennsylvania. Henry Francis du Pont Winterthur Museum, Winterthur, Del.

12.
Mahogany Chippendale-style tall clock with a movement by the eminent Philadelphia clockmaker Edward Duffield. Note the applied hood carving and base panel on the magnificently crafted case. American, Philadelphia, 1765–75. Henry Francis du Pont Winterthur Museum, Winterthur, Del.

13.
Queen Anne tall clock by George Graham, one of the greatest of the great eighteenth-century English horologists. The case is walnut and has pierced fretwork on an atypical hood midway between a flat top and a step top. English, London, c. 1715. Metropolitan Museum of Art, New York, gift of Irwin Untermyer, 1964

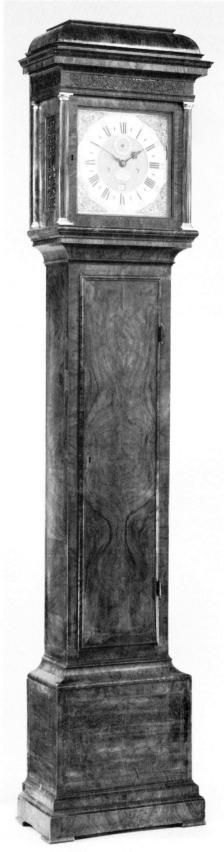

12

13

a scroll pediment with very bold rosettes, and turned pillars at each corner of the hood. The waist has fluted quarter columns and line inlay; the base, additional inlay and French bracket feet. The dial is painted on iron, and there is an age-of-the-moon attachment in the dial arch. The two winding holes, as already indicated, show that it is an eight-day clock. The notable feature of this particular dial is the set of four hands, all pivoted in the center. The shorter of the two hands on the right, the one pointing to 3, is a brass calendar hand; the long steel hand pointing to 6 is a *center seconds hand*. The center seconds hand is found on a number of Pennsylvania tall clocks. To make provision for it, the wheels in the movement are so arranged that the escape wheel (whose arbor carries the seconds hand) is much lower in the movement than it would otherwise be. Rather than an anchor, or recoil, escapement, the escapement here is a *deadbeat escapement*, which was designed to avoid the recoil of the other.

Two additional Pennsylvania tall clocks are illustrated in colorplate 4 and plate 12. Also illustrated (plate 13) is a clock that despite its atypical hood design may fairly be called a representative example of the early eighteenth-century English tall clocks (or long-case clocks, as they are known in England) that so clearly influenced later American styles.

14.
Round-top mahogany and cherry bracket clock by Frederick Heisely. Its center calendar hand and pinwheel escapement are unusual features. The indicator on the STRIKE/SILENT dial in the arch is moved by hand to activate or silence the strike. American, Harrisburg, Pennsylvania, c. 1830. Private collection

Colorplate 5.
English eight-day bracket clock by the Brockbank firm of London. This typical brass-mounted ebony-veneered example, dating from about 1770, carries a calendar dial in the arch. The maker is probably John Brockbank. Private collection

Colorplate 6.
Clock in colorplate 5: rear view, showing the bell, bob pendulum and engraved backplate of the movement

Another type of English clock that contributed to the American horological heritage is the *bracket clock*, a spring-driven clock intended for a table, mantel, shelf or special wall bracket. Such clocks appeared in England about 1670 and were made, with variations and improvements, throughout most of the eighteenth century (colorplates 5 and 6). The sides and back of a bracket-clock case were made largely of glass, so that the fine workmanship of the movement could be admired.

Only a few bracket clocks were made in America, most of them direct copies of English examples. An American bracket clock that dared to be a little different (plate 14) was made by Frederick Heisely (1759–1843) of Harrisburg, Pennsylvania, about 1830. The case shows

15

15.
Flat-top thirty-hour walnut tall clock by Jacob Mollinger. Some of the characteristics of its movement, hands and dial appear later in clocks by George Hoff, a German immigrant who was established in Lancaster, Pennsylvania, by 1769 and who worked there as a clockmaker until his death in 1816. German, Neustadt, mid-eighteenth century. Private collection

16.
Eight-day wag-on-the-wall clock with the side door opened to show the mechanism. The movement is characteristically set in a wooden frame, with solid wooden plates top and bottom and flat wooden posts to support the arbors. The wheels are brass, and the arbors are steel. As with most such clocks, this example is unsigned. South German, nineteenth century. Private collection

Colorplate 7.
Modified pillar-and-scroll wooden shelf clock by an unknown maker. Its thirty-hour movement is similar to that of a German wag-on-the-wall. American, eastern Pennsylvania, c. 1830. Private collection

16

Colorplate 8.
Pinewood Queen Anne–style tall clock by
Gawen Brown (1719–1801), considered by
some authorities to have the finest American
japanned case in existence. The japanning
was probably done by Thomas Johnson.
Note the rocking ship in the dial arch; this
is a decorative device attached to a pendulum that "rocks" as the pendulum swings.
Boston, 1750–55. Henry Francis du Pont
Winterthur Museum, Winterthur, Del.

some obvious departures from the English prototype, including even a ninety-degree turn of the top handle.

The German influence on tall-clock styles was most directly felt in southeastern Pennsylvania, especially in Lancaster County. Several makers of that area produced clocks obviously based on those of Jacob Mollinger of Neustadt, Germany (plate 15). The full story of the connection between the clocks of Neustadt and those of Lancaster County is still being investigated.

Germany's Black Forest region produced a distinctive wall clock (a typical example is shown in plate 16) that was later reflected in some Pennsylvania clocks. Brought to America from Germany in the eighteenth and nineteenth centuries, this type of clock could be mounted on the wall without the benefit of a case and became known as a *wag-on-the-wall*. Immigrants who carried the clocks with them to America frequently had cases built by a local carpenter after they arrived. The style and quality of the cases vary widely. Often the "wags" were set into tall-clock cases, and today they frequently appear with a tag reading "Pennsylvania tall clock" but it should be remembered that only the case is Pennsylvanian, not the mechanism.

The wag movement was modified by one or more enterprising Pennsylvania clockmakers in the 1830s and incorporated into a Pennsylvania version of the pillar-and-scroll clock (colorplate 7). The case is a Germanic interpretation of the lovely clock shown in colorplate 1 (see page 12). The bracket feet have become turned feet. The scrolls are less delicate, and the finials are of turned wood. The dial is iron and the lower door tablet is painted tin under clear glass.

During the decade 1830–40 a small number of the modified pillar-and-scroll and other shelf clocks were made in Pennsylvania. Handcrafted, they could not compete commercially with the less expensive products of the Connecticut clock factories. A heroic example by Thomas Weaver of Milheim stands almost 4 feet (121.9 centimeters) tall (plate 17). This clock, with eclectic styling related to the Connecticut pillar and scroll as well as to later Connecticut designs, was completed on November 11, 1838.

The end of the shelf-clock effort in Pennsylvania about 1840 marked the end of serious clockmaking in that state. Neither the craft nor the industry prospered in Pennsylvania thereafter.

New England Clocks   Clockmakers could be found in many parts of the New England colonies in the early eighteenth century, and all made tall clocks for local consumption. As the century progressed, the types ranged from rather primitive clocks from Maine to elegant products from Newport or Boston (colorplate 8), and generally followed English inspiration. The case styles reflected not only the tastes and desires of the purchasers but the constraints imposed by the prevailing domestic architecture. Homes of modest size, with

17.
Large wooden shelf clock, nearly 4 feet (121.9 centimeters) high, by Thomas Weaver. Its eclectic design incorporates a stenciled crest, moon dial, center-section columns and bracket feet with skirt; its well-finished eight-day movement indicates its maker had English training. American, Milheim, Pennsylvania, 1838. Private collection

18

19

20

18.
Mahogany dwarf tall clock, only 66 inches
(167.6 centimeters) high, by Thomas Clag-
gett. Miniature versions of larger clocks are
generally quite rare. American, Newport,
Rhode Island, 1730–49.

19.
Mahogany tall clock with an iron and brass
movement by David Williams and a painted
iron dial by James Wilson. The case reflects
the artistry of the renowned Newport cabinetmaker John Townsend—note the shell-
carved block-front waist door, the stopped
fluting on the hood pillars and waist quarter
columns, the corkscrew and reeded urn
finials and the ogee bracket feet. American,
Newport, Rhode Island, 1770–85.

20.
Simon Willard mahogany tall clock with the
so-called Roxbury case. It features inlaid
quarter fans on the waist door, brass capitals
and brass stopped fluting on the hood pillars
and waist quarter columns, and ogee bracket
feet. American, Roxbury, Massachusetts,
1790–1815.

21.
Thirty-hour brass-dial mahogany wall clock
by Simon Willard. This early effort of
Willard's represents some of the experi-
mental work that culminated about twenty
years later in his hugely successful banjo
clock. American, Roxbury, Massachusetts,
c. 1780.

The clocks in plates 18–21 are from the
Henry Francis du Pont Winterthur Museum,
Winterthur, Del.

22.
Mahogany Massachusetts shelf clock by
Aaron Willard. The distinguishing design
feature of the elegantly simple case is the
kidney-shaped bonnet. American, Boston, c.
1800. Metropolitan Museum of Art, New
York, Sylmaris Collection, gift of George
Coe Graves, 1930

21

22

ceilings built low to make heating easier, could find space only for smaller clocks (plate 18), while high-ceilinged mansions could accommodate the tall and distinguished cabinetwork (plate 19) of such eighteenth-century craftsmen as Job Townsend (1699–1765), his nephew John Townsend (b. 1733) and his apprentice and son-in-law John Goddard (1723–1785)—all members of the celebrated Townsend-Goddard dynasty of Newport furniture makers.

New England clockmaking as a craft reached its peak in Massachusetts, thanks in large degree to the Willard family, especially Simon Willard, regarded by many as the dean of American clockmakers. Born in Grafton, Massachusetts, in 1753, Simon was the second of four Willard brothers to achieve fame as clockmakers, the others being Benjamin (1743–1803), Ephraim (b. 1755) and Aaron (1757–1844). Details of Simon's early training are not well documented, but it is believed that he went to work for his elder brother, Benjamin, after having been apprenticed to a clockmaker from England. Certainly his tall clocks reflect a strong English influence. An inventive and conscientious craftsman, he died in 1848 at the age of ninety-five.

The Simon Willard tall clock shown in plate 20 was made after Simon moved from Grafton to Roxbury, a suburb of Boston. The case style is so closely identified with his work in Roxbury that it is now called a Roxbury case. The proportions of Roxbury cases are excellent. They have a slender and graceful waist, a round-top hood, three finials with chimneys, and fretwork between. The finials are usually brass ball-and-spire, and the commonest fretting is a delicate, almost lacy, pierced crest. The dial is painted on iron, a style introduced in England about the time of the American Revolution. The *white dial*, as it was called, quickly became popular in both England and America, and the transition from brass dials to painted white dials was quite abrupt. As a rule, tall clocks with brass dials, except those from Connecticut, are pre-Revolutionary; those with white dials, post-Revolutionary. The white dial is the more readable, but the real reason for its rapid acceptance was that it cost less than the brass one.

Simon Willard and his brother Aaron were responsible for the introduction of a clock style that would quickly become a staple and that remains a staple even today. In 1802 Simon secured a patent on what he called an "Improved Timepiece," a wall clock later known as a *banjo clock*. A good Willard banjo clock is typically an eight-day, weight-driven timepiece with a movement made entirely of brass and steel and a case consisting of three main sections: the *head*, or *hood*; the *throat*, or middle section; and the *box*, or base (colorplate 9).

The popularity of the banjo clock was so great that other makers soon copied it, and over the years a substantial number of the clocks

23.
Mahogany and white pine Massachusetts shelf clock by Daniel Balch, Jr. (1761–1835). The reeded pilasters, sophisticated scrolls and finials, and handsome base panel and moldings add up to an exceptional case. American, Newburyport, Massachusetts, 1790–95. Henry Francis du Pont Winterthur Museum, Winterthur, Del.

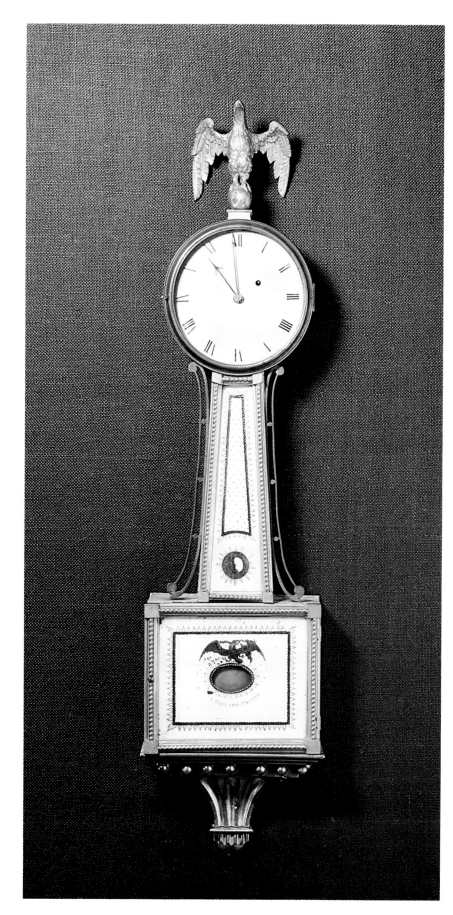

Colorplate 9.
Simon Willard banjo clock of mahogany and pine painted white, with side arms of pierced brass. This version is called a bride's clock, white symbolizing purity. The glass panel in the base is signed *Willard and Nolen*, for Aaron Willard, Jr. (1783–1864), and his brother-in-law, Spencer Nolen, who at the time were in business together as ornamental painters. American, Roxbury, Massachusetts, 1802–10. Henry Francis du Pont Winterthur Museum, Winterthur, Del.

were produced. As with other successful designs, the temptation to improve it was irresistible, and almost immediately variants appeared. The most spectacular of these was the highly gilded version called the *girandole* (see frontispiece) that was made by Lemuel Curtis (b. 1790), a nephew and apprentice of Aaron Willard's. This clock is truly a bold expression of a new style in a new nation, whatever one thinks of its innate beauty—or lack of it.

Two earlier non-tall clocks from Massachusetts are associated with the Willard brothers. Simon made a small thirty-hour wall clock (plate 21) that bore little resemblance to his later banjo clock but did testify to his innovative skills. He and Aaron also made what is known as the *Massachusetts shelf clock*. This is an eight-day, weight-driven clock with a brass and steel movement and pendulum regulation. It is, in some respects, a scaled-down tall clock. Massachusetts shelf-clock cases, in contrast with the prevailing tall-clock styles, have only two sections; the waist is missing (plates 22 and 23). Unlike the banjo clocks, which often do not carry their maker's name, the Massachusetts shelf clocks are usually signed.

The banjo clock and the Massachusetts shelf clock were the only two non-tall clocks made in quantity in America before the pillar-and-scroll clock. Neither was made "to a price," as was the pillar and scroll. The banjo design had a lasting impact on American horology and was a commercial success for Simon Willard. Massachusetts shelf clocks continued to be made in the early nineteenth century, but competition from banjo and pillar-and-scroll clocks led to their demise.

Connecticut clockmaking, as we know, was a flourishing business. In the eighteenth century, Connecticut clocks were of two types: tall clocks with brass movements and tall clocks with wooden movements. Those with brass movements are rarer and generally earlier than those with wood. Fine examples of the former came from the shop of the English-born clockmaker Thomas Harland, who immigrated to Boston in 1773. He soon removed to Norwich, Connecticut, where he began a successful trade as a clockmaker and where he later trained other craftsmen. (As we have seen, Eli Terry was apprenticed to a Harland-trained clockmaker.) Unlike later wooden-movement clocks, such brass-movement tall clocks were usually sold

24.
Brass-movement tall clock by Thomas Harland. The solid cherry Norwich case shows the typical whale's-tails cresting, fluted chimneys and full hood columns found on this type of case, but the bracket feet are unusual. American, Norwich, Connecticut, c. 1774. Private collection

with cases. They were not made with cost-cutting measures in mind, but rather—in the spirit of the best English clockmaking—with the intention of producing sound, functional clocks in cases pleasing to the eye.

The case of the Harland clock illustrated in plate 24 is a fine example of a style that became popular in Norwich and is now known as a Norwich case. Such cases have round-top hoods and three turned wooden finials mounted on fluted chimneys. The hood edge between the finials is filled with a delicately carved crest in the fretwork design often referred to as "whale's tails" because the carving suggests that nautical image. These cases usually have ogee feet, so called because in cross section they show S-shaped, or ogival, curves. (For a closeup view of the clockface, see colorplate 2, page 22.)

A singular type of wooden-movement tall clock was made in Connecticut between about 1770 and 1830. This clock was a direct result of local economic conditions. As already noted, brass was scarce during the years following the Revolution, and clocks made with it were expensive. In an effort to produce a clock for buyers of modest means, Connecticut makers designed and built movements of local woods. These clocks usually ran only one day on a winding, though some eight-day examples are known. What the buyer got for his money was a movement, dial, hands, pendulum and weight shells. The shells were empty metal cylinders to be filled with sand, stone, metal scrap or whatever would make them heavy enough to serve as weights. These clocks were often carried on their travels by the ubiquitous Yankee peddlers, and the sales they made throughout the American countryside helped Connecticut become the center of the mid-nine-teenth-century clock industry.

Once a buyer had procured such a clock, he had to have a case built to house it. He could contract with a local cabinetmaker to construct a piece of some quality or call upon a local coffinmaker. Or he could do the work himself. Consequently, many kinds of cases are found with these clocks, varying greatly in style and workmanship (plate 25). The earliest such clocks had brass dials. Then came wooden dials, pasted over with paper on which the chapter ring was printed. Still others have the chapter ring and sundry decorations painted directly on a wooden dial board. If the clockmaker chose to

25.
Thirty-hour wooden-movement tall clock by Riley Whiting (1785–1835). The gracefully proportioned case is pine with artificial graining, and the bold molding between waist and base is clearly the work of a skilled if unknown cabinetmaker. American, Winchester, Connecticut, c. 1820. Private collection

put his name on the clock, he put it somewhere on the dial, but many clocks were left unsigned.

From about 1810 until nearly 1820, production of these wooden tall clocks was at its peak. It stopped completely about a decade after the introduction of Terry's pillar-and-scroll clock, the success of which, as has been said, signaled a dramatic change in the American clock business. This change was relatively abrupt in Connecticut, where the production of all but shelf clocks tapered off very quickly. The change came more slowly elsewhere, but within twenty years Connecticut's new industry put most of the country's individual craftsmen out of business and became a virtual monopoly. Massachusetts clockmakers had already abandoned the tall clock for the new and fashionable banjo clock made by the Willards and others. Clockmakers elsewhere plied their trade briefly but were unable to compete with the mass-produced products, and by 1850 the Connecticut industry in effect had the field to itself.

Imitation may be the sincerest form of flattery, but when economic issues are involved, imitation is often called plagiarism and legal actions are likely to result. So it was with the pillar-and-scroll clock. Terry was enough of a businessman to protect himself with a series of patents on his shelf clock, but some of his competitors found ways to modify the Terry clock so as to circumvent his patents. Others simply infringed. At first, Terry allowed the fruit of his invention to be plucked by others. A good example of this is the *box clock* (plate 26) manufactured under license from Terry by Seth Thomas (1785–1859), a joiner who had earlier been in Terry's employ and who later set up a Connecticut clock factory of his own. The box clock, a design Terry discarded on the way to developing the pillar and scroll, is essentially a pillar-and-scroll clock minus scroll, pillars, bracket feet, skirt and finials. Instead of a painted wooden dial mounted between the movement and the glass of the door, it has the hour circle painted on the back of the door glass. The hands are affixed to the movement in the usual manner but actually rotate behind the dial instead of in front of it. It is simply what the name implies—a clock in a box.

The two decades following the introduction of the pillar-and-scroll clock saw other Connecticut clockmakers besides Thomas vying for success in the new industry Terry had fathered. The wooden-movement shelf clock was supreme, and these were its finest years. Interesting variations on both case style and movement began to appear. One of the most colorful was produced by Chauncey Jerome (1793–1868), a joiner and budding entrepreneur who in 1827 introduced what he called a *bronze looking-glass clock* (plate 27), proudly claiming that his design was both artistically superior to and cheaper to manufacture than the pillar and scroll. In fact, not only

26.
Mahogany-veneered box clock by Seth Thomas. This variation on Eli Terry's pillar-and-scroll clock utilized an early Terry "strap" movement in which strips of wood were used instead of solid wooden plates. American, Plymouth, Connecticut, 1816–18. American Clock and Watch Museum, Bristol, Conn.

was it manufactured for one dollar less, it was sold for two dollars more, a situation dear to the budding entrepreneur's heart, but its contribution to the decorative arts is open to debate.

The movement in Chauncey Jerome's clock was designed by Noble Jerome (1800–1861), his brother and business partner. It is noticeably thinner (that is, there is less distance between the movement plates) than any other wooden movement of the time, and the case likewise is shallower than most. The door, which is the entire front of the clock, accounts for a substantial part of the total weight, however, so that the clock tends to fall on its face when the door is opened. The clock is also top-heavy when the weights have been wound up; consequently, it must be secured to a shelf or wall or it will meet with early catastrophe. The pendulum is so long that it nearly scrapes the bottom of the case, making proper regulation difficult, if not impossible. In short, this clock was an engineering disaster.

Stylistically, in spite of its faults, it pointed the way to less expensive cases with designs stenciled on half columns. The term *bronze looking-glass clock* does not refer to a special method for production of the mirror. The "bronze" refers to the bronze powders

27.
Typical bronze looking-glass clock, with wooden case and movement, made by the firm of Jeromes & Darrow. It has a mirror tablet and bronze-stenciled half columns and crest. American, Bristol, Connecticut, c. 1827. Private collection

28.
Miniature (24¾ inches, or 62.9 centimeters, high) thirty-hour wooden-movement timepiece with alarm by Putnam Bailey, appropriately adorned with a crowing cock. In addition to the carved rooster crest, the wooden case also has carved half columns and feet. American, Goshen, Connecticut, c. 1835. American Clock and Watch Museum, Bristol, Conn.

29.
Wooden shelf clock by Silas Hoadley (1786–1870) with an upside-down wooden movement (note the winding-hole positions). The case has a shell-and-foliage-carved crest and

27

28

stenciled quarter columns; the front feet are carved and the back ones turned. The motto in the tablet reminds us that "time is money." American, Plymouth, Connecticut, c. 1830. Private collection

30.
Reeded-pilaster-and-scroll wooden shelf clock, with a thirty-hour wooden movement, by Jeromes & Darrow. Unlike the original Terry pillar and scroll, this reeded pilaster version does not have bracket feet or a base skirt. American, Bristol, Connecticut, 1825–30. Private collection

31.
Wooden-cased eight-day brass-movement New Hampshire mirror timepiece, typically framed with gilded half columns, by Benjamin Morrill (1794–1857). American, Boscawen, New Hampshire, c. 1820. Private collection

used instead of gold leaf in the stenciling. The case could be made more cheaply than that of the earlier pillar-and-scroll clock for several reasons. To begin with, the graceful scroll of the latter was replaced with a simple stenciled crest. The finials and backboard extension were eliminated, as were the feet and skirt. In place of the turned pillars a single turned pillar was split and applied to each side of the door, and, finally, the reverse-painted tablet was supplanted by an undecorated mirror.

The half-column case was sometimes carved rather than stenciled, and doubtless this work was relatively expensive to execute. Occasionally both half columns and crest were carved (plate 28), with crest carvings rather grandly done. The net effect was an elegant if heavy case. One sometimes finds a case (plate 29) where stenciling and carving have been combined.

Another variant on the pillar-and-scroll case worth special mention is the *reeded pilaster and scroll* (plate 30). Here scroll and finials have been retained, but the turned pillars have been replaced by flat, reeded sections attached to the front of the clock. Feet and skirt are gone, and the tablet has become part tablet and part metal plate (now

29

30

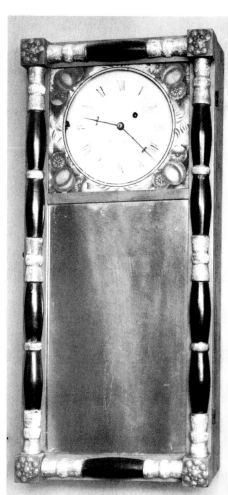

31

usually much worn). It is not uncommon to find only a mirror used.

Although the clocks made in Connecticut after 1820 far outnumber those from other parts of the United States, a few interesting examples were made elsewhere. In Massachusetts, Simon Willard's banjo clock continued in popularity. In neighboring New Hampshire, a banjo-like clock in a radically different case appeared. This *New Hampshire mirror clock* (plate 31) has a simple box for a case; a mirror fills most of the door, and the door takes up the entire front. Gilded half columns are used around the door's edges, and above the mirror is a reverse-painted tablet with an aperture for the dial. The movements of these clocks are mostly brass and nearly always quite small, and frequently the plates are severely cut out to save as much brass as possible. The pendulum hangs down between the dial and the movement, as in the pillar-and-scroll and banjo clocks (unlike the typical tall clock, in which the pendulum hangs between the backplate of the movement and the backboard of the case), and wires are sometimes strung vertically inside the case to prevent the weight from interfering with the pendulum.

The use of a mirror to fill most of the front of a clock was not exclusive with New Hampshire. In 1822 Joseph Ives (1782–1862) of Connecticut obtained a patent on a clockcase dominated by a mirror. This Ives clock (plate 32) stands quite high—52 inches (132.1 centimeters)—because it uses a seconds-beating pendulum, which is about 39 inches (99.1 centimeters) long. A tablet above the mirror reveals the dial, and the pendulum bob can be seen through the tablet below the mirror.

Ives was an inventive genius as a clockmaker but a failure as a businessman. His career, which began in 1810, spanned fifty-two years, and he produced a series of remarkable innovations, many of which resulted in clocks that are highly prized by today's collectors. But for all his ability, he invented nothing that outlived him by more than a few years. An example of the last clock design to incorporate an Ives invention (the *roller pinions* in the movement) is seen in plate 33.

In the early 1830s large, eight-day brass-movement shelf clocks began to appear in some quantity in central Connecticut, the land of wooden-movement clocks. Many of these had movements based on Ives designs that Ives had allowed others to use in return for their helping him out of financial difficulties. The cases of these clocks are often called Empire cases and may be further distinguished as double-deckers or triple-deckers, depending on whether they have two or three distinct sections. On a typical double-decker, which is sectioned by two doors, the upper door is ordinarily about twice the size of the lower and is usually itself in two parts, one for the dial and one for a tablet. The lower door may also have a tablet of some sort. On a triple-decker (plate 34), the upper door usually covers only the dial and is

32.
Large wooden mirror clock, more than 4 feet (132.1 centimeters) high, by Joseph Ives. The case carries a scroll crest and finials heavier and larger than those on Terry's pillar-and-scroll clock. (The finials here are not the originals.) American, Bristol, Connecticut, 1820–25. Private collection

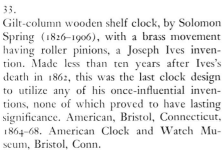

33.
Gilt-column wooden shelf clock, by Solomon Spring (1826–1906), with a brass movement having roller pinions, a Joseph Ives invention. Made less than ten years after Ives's death in 1862, this was the last clock design to utilize any of his once-influential inventions, none of which proved to have lasting significance. American, Bristol, Connecticut, 1864–68. American Clock and Watch Museum, Bristol, Conn.

34.
Brass-movement shelf clock in a wooden triple-decker Empire case with gilding. Stenciled letters on the crest identify the maker as the firm of C. & L. C. Ives, "C" being Chauncey Ives, brother of Joseph, and "L. C." being Lawson C. Ives, a nephew. The pendulum bob swings behind the heart-shaped aperture in the lower tablet. American, Bristol, Connecticut, 1833–37. American Clock and Watch Museum, Bristol, Conn.

35   36

35.
Eight-day wooden-movement shelf clock by
Jeromes & Darrow. The wooden case fea-
tures a three-section single door, and it
has the carved splat and half columns
frequently seen on clocks of this type.
American, Bristol, Connecticut, 1830–35.
Private collection

36.
Giant mahogany-veneered hollow-column
shelf clock, 44 inches (111.8 centimeters)
high, marketed by J. J. Beals of Boston.
In addition to time and strike trains, the
thirty-hour wooden movement has an alarm
mechanism. American, Connecticut, c. 1840.
Private collection

separated from the lower by a nonoperable middle section with a
painted tablet or mirror.

In the early 1830s, furthermore, Connecticut wooden-movement
clocks, far from being abandoned by their makers, were produced in
various new forms. Since most brass-movement clocks were eight-day
clocks, and since winding a clock once a week is obviously more con-
venient than winding it once a day, eight-day wooden movements
were introduced (plate 35). The additional power required meant
that cases had to be taller and weights heavier. Greater demands were
placed on the wooden gearing—demands that such gearing was not
always able to meet, so stripped teeth and pinion leaves were not uncommon.

The continuing search for new case designs during the 1830s produced the so-called *hollow-column clock* (plate 36). In this intriguing
clock the weights descend through the oversize hollow columns on
either side of the upper part of the case. There is, however, no useful

purpose served by the design unless keeping the weights hidden can be considered useful; and if a need for repairs arises while the weights are inside the columns, the whole arrangement becomes a nuisance.

In the late 1830s, a scant twenty years after Eli Terry introduced his pillar-and-scroll clock, two innovations combined to effect a dramatic change in clockmaking—a change that would eventually bring to an end the production of all wooden-movement clocks. These were the design of an inexpensive rolled-brass clock movement and the introduction of springs to replace weights as the source of power.

The Connecticut clock industry had been seriously affected by the Panic of 1837, as had industry throughout the United States; and one of those who sought to revive the faltering clock business was the same Chauncey Jerome who had brought out the bronze looking-glass clock in 1827. In 1839 U.S. Patent No. 1200 was issued to his brother, Noble Jerome, for the "striking parts of a clock." Actually, what Noble had succeeded in designing was a thirty-hour brass movement that could be made out of the relatively inexpensive rolled brass then becoming available, in particular from mills in lower-central Connecticut. Capitalizing on Patent No. 1200, Chauncey and Noble Jerome began to manufacture rolled-brass movements, and within a

37.
Two mahogany-veneered ogee clocks by Chauncey Jerome. The clock on the right has a mirror tablet; the one on the left, a transfer print. The expensive reverse-painted tablet is rarely found in an ogee; a transfer print, etched glass or mirror tablet is used instead. Right: Bristol, Connecticut, 1840–45. Left: New Haven, Connecticut, 1845–50. Private collection

short time installed them in ogee cases (plate 37)—and the career of the most successful American weight-driven clock (made in large numbers through 1900) was under way. The name of the style derives from the ogee molding (molding that in profile follows an S-shaped, or ogival, curve) that forms the entire front of the clock except for the door. At the time, the ogee shape was extremely fashionable and designers found ways to use it as often as possible.

The use of coiled springs instead of weights to power American clocks had a similarly strong and nearly simultaneous impact on the industry. Coiled springs in clocks were not new; they had been employed by European clockmakers since the mid-fifteenth century. But springs had never been widely available on this side of the Atlantic, although a few spring-driven clocks were made—for example, the early bracket clocks. These, however, used imported springs and were always individually handcrafted. One early attempt at manufacturing spring-driven clocks in some quantity was made by the Plymouth, Connecticut, firm of Curtiss & Clark, which produced a few hundred clocks with imported springs in the mid-1820s (colorplate 10). The clocks were successful but the business apparently was not, for production soon stopped. It was evidently impossible to compete with the rising flood of cheap wooden clocks from Connecticut at that time.

The introduction of springs offered two important benefits to the clockmaker: He could make his clocks smaller (no need for height to accommodate a weight drop) and he could make his clocks lighter and more portable. The desire for portability led to the design of clocks governed by *balance wheels* instead of pendulums, since a pendulum-controlled clock could not operate while being carried or shifted about but had to be kept upright and in a fixed position. The use of an oscillating wheel, called a balance wheel, to control the escape wheel allowed construction of a clock that could operate in various positions. These clocks could be used in nonstationary locations, such as on boats. In fact, the first balance-wheel clocks were called *marine clocks* to emphasize their usefulness at sea.

There is still considerable mystery about who designed the first successful American-made coiled-spring-driven clock, an example of which is shown in plate 38. The case of this clock was obviously meant to hold a spring-driven movement, since there is no provision for weight drop. When produced, it was called a *round Gothic clock*, for its rounded Gothic arch (the Gothic Revival style was then much in vogue in both England and America), but now it is known as a *beehive clock*, in recognition of its overall shape. Each of its gear trains, like those of a number of other early spring-driven clocks, contains a device called a *fusee*. This is a conical, spirally wound pulley located between the spring and the first wheel of the

Colorplate 10.
Carved wooden eight-day shelf clock powered by coiled springs imported from Geneva, Switzerland. Made by the firm of Curtiss & Clark, it is one of the earliest spring-powered clocks manufactured in the United States. American, Plymouth, Connecticut, c. 1825. Private collection

38.
Round Gothic, or beehive, clock, the first commercially successful spring-driven clock produced in America. This rosewood-veneered example, with its unique zinc dial, may have been made by the firm of E. C. Brewster. American, Connecticut, c. 1841. Private collection

39.
Clock in colorplate 11 with the door opened, revealing the strike gong (the spiral wire below the dial), pendulum, label and fusees. The springs, which are behind the fusees, are not visible here.

Colorplate 11.
Fusee-spring-driven acorn clock by the Forestville Manufacturing Company of Jonathan Clark Brown (1807–1872). The clock was named for the acorn shape of the upper section of the case and the knobs on the ends of the side arms. The case of this example is laminated wood. (The painting is a modern reproduction.) American, Bristol, Connecticut, c. 1848. Private collection

MERCHANTS' EXCHANGE
PHILADELPHIA

gear train. The fusee is connected to the first wheel by a cord, chain or piece of gut that unwinds during the running of the clock. The original function of the fusee—and the device was known in Europe at least as early as 1450—was to deliver a constant torque to the gear train even though the pull exerted by the coiled spring varied with its state of tension. Since the first American-made springs exerted a notably irregular pull, this function was a primary one. But fusees in American clocks performed a curious secondary function as well. They allowed clockmakers to use weight-driven movements with little change as they moved into the spring-clock business. A weight-driven clock requires only that a cord under tension supply power to the first wheel of the gear train. There is no change in the functioning of the movement if that tension is supplied by a coiled spring rather than a weight. A number of early American spring-driven clocks were constructed by designing a movement with spring and fusee that put tension on a cord that had previously supported a weight.

In early fusee clocks, springs and fusees were located near either the middle or the base of the clock, separate from the movement. Although it was made somewhat later, this is still the arrangement in J. C. Brown's *acorn clock* (colorplate 11), one of the more fanciful American clockcase designs. When the door is open, the fusees—one for the time train, one for the strike—are visible at the bottom of the case (plate 39). The corresponding springs are located directly behind the fusees.

The years from 1840 to 1860 saw many experiments in spring clocks and the appearance of a number of interesting types. Some were produced only briefly and are of importance today only to collectors. On the other hand, some that emerged had spring-driven movements that would endure with only minor changes for the next hundred years.

The first manufacturer to recognize the coming trend toward the spring-driven clock was Elisha Curtis Brewster of Connecticut. About 1842 he began making an eight-day spring movement that was patented in 1843 by Charles Kirk. The backplate of this movement was cast iron, with well-like depressions to house the springs. Early springs broke rather easily, and the wells protected the rest of the movement from the effects of a rupture. The first of these movements was placed in a round Gothic case. In 1844 Brewster formed a partnership with the Ingraham brothers, Elias (1805–1885) and Andrew, and the well-known *sharp Gothic clock* appeared. Elias Ingraham became famous as a case designer; probably his most celebrated design is the sharp Gothic, later called the *steeple* (colorplate 12).

Colorplate 12.
Left: round Gothic, or beehive, clock by E. C. Brewster, 1843. Right: sharp Gothic, or steeple, clock by Brewster & Ingrahams, 1844. The beehive has a wooden dial with a gilded hour ring; the steeple has a painted zinc dial. Both clocks are of wood with eight-day iron-backplate spring movements and engraved tablets. American, Bristol, Connecticut. Private collection

Joseph Ives had experimented with clocks powered by other than weights as early as the 1820s. Between 1825 and 1830, while temporarily located in Brooklyn, New York, he had made clocks powered by a bent steel strap fastened in the base of the case. Cords attached to the ends of this strap were wound onto the first wheel arbor, which was thickened to form a drum. The energy released as the bent strap straightened supplied the power. Like many other Ives ventures, this one had not been financially successful, and it was at this point that Ives had been put back on his feet by the group of clockmakers who had used his brass movements in the Empire cases of the early 1830s. Around 1840 he needed rescuing again, and his rescuers

40.
Eight-day wagon-spring clock designed by Joseph Ives and made by Birge & Fuller in a wooden double-candlestick case. The box-like lower section of the case houses the wagon-spring mechanism; the dial and movement proper are in the upper section. The tablets are decorated with openwork transfers. American, Bristol, Connecticut, 1844–48. Private collection

41.
Clock in plate 40 with the doors opened to show the spring mechanism. The label gives directions for adjusting the clock if it should run fast or slow.

42

43

42.
Mahogany-veneered thirty-hour triple-fusee steeple clock by Chauncey Boardman, probably made for export to Quebec. (Note the picture in the tablet is entitled MARKET PLACE QUEBEC.) The term triple fusee refers to the fact that each of the clock's three trains—time, strike and alarm—has a fusee in it. American, Bristol, Connecticut, c. 1850. American Clock and Watch Museum, Bristol, Conn.

43.
Glorified eight-day wooden steeple clock with four columns and applied ripple molding, by Brewster & Ingrahams. Four-column steeples with planar tops and without rippling are also found. American, Bristol, Connecticut, c. 1850. American Clock and Watch Museum, Bristol, Conn.

brought out another of his designs, this one representing the second generation of clocks he had designed in Brooklyn. Ives called this clock the *accelerating lever spring clock*, but today it is known as the *wagon spring* (plates 40 and 41).

The tablet on the triple-fusee steeple clock by Chauncey Boardman (1789–1857) shown in plate 42 portrays a scene in Quebec. This scene serves to illustrate a significant side of the American clock business—the export side. In the early 1840s Chauncey Jerome began to ship his brass-movement ogees to England, where they were offered for sale at substantially lower prices than the finely made English products demanded. English customs officials attempted to stop this aspect of Jerome's business but failed, and in due course he established an active overseas market. His success soon led others to follow, and by 1865 American clocks were being shipped by the thousands to more than thirty countries. Clocks prepared for sale outside the United States were often fitted with tablets intended to appeal to foreign customers. Boardman's triple-fusee steeple clock was probably made for sale by a distributor in or near Quebec.

The most elaborate version of Elias Ingraham's simple steeple clock is one carrying four freestanding pillars and finials (plate 43). The upper portion of the case is not constructed of planes but of S-curves culminating in a point, giving the clock a sort of onion-top appearance. Much of the front surface has an applied ripple molding quite popular in the 1850s. A full name for this style might be four-pillar, ripple-front, Oriental sharp Gothic.

The new freedom afforded by the use of springs rather than weights allowed the development of the small and simple *gallery clock* (plate 44), so called because of its frequent use on the front of a gallery in an auditorium or church. Actually, weight-driven gallery clocks had been made by such earlier clockmakers as Simon Willard, but they were large, costly affairs, while the spring-driven gallery clocks of the 1850 era were made for a mass market. These are found with two sorts of movements. One is a spring-driven pendulum movement, usually without a striking mechanism. The other is a spring-driven balance-wheel movement that did not appear until shortly before 1850. Most early gallery clocks are painted or gilded; later ones commonly have a varnished natural surface. At first they had round cases, but within a few years octagonal cases became popular and after that square ones. The firm of Brewster & Ingrahams even created a banjo version of its gallery clock (plate 45).

Yet another style developed from the octagonal gallery clock (plate 46). A small box was added to the bottom of the case to accommodate a pendulum slightly longer than the normal gallery

44.
Brewster & Ingrahams gilt-wood gallery timepiece with an eight-day iron-backplate pendulum-controlled spring movement. This
style had no dial glass. American, Bristol,
Connecticut, c. 1850. Private collection

45.
The first American spring-driven time-piece, a product of Brewster & Ingrahams. This variation on the gallery clock is made of wood and has a pendulum-controlled movement. American, Bristol, Connecticut, c. 1850. Private collection

46.
Mahogany-veneered octagon drop clock by Chauncey Jerome. This early example contains an eight-day fusee timepiece, an unusual movement for a clock of this type. American, New Haven, Connecticut, c. 1850. American Clock and Watch Museum, Bristol, Conn.

45

46

47

47.
American Clock Company's "baseball" clock showing likenesses of real players. Behind the decorative cast-iron front is a plain wooden box containing the movement. American, New York City, 1875–80. Private collection

48.
Wooden parlor calendar clock made by the E. Ingraham Company. All models of this popular clock accounted for the different lengths of the months; some accounted for leap years as well. American, Bristol, Connecticut, 1882–94. American Clock and Watch Museum, Bristol, Conn.

49.
One of the E. Ingraham Company's Army-Navy line of six shelf clocks commemorating military heroes. This model features Admiral Dewey on its pressed-oak crest. American, Bristol, Connecticut, 1898–1900. American Clock and Watch Museum, Bristol, Conn.

50.
Gilded cast-metal shelf clock by the Ansonia Clock Company. One of the so-called figurine clocks for which Ansonia became well known, this example was directly inspired by contemporary French styles. American, Brooklyn, New York, 1880–90. American Clock and Watch Museum, Bristol, Conn.

pendulum. This clock was initially known as an *octagon drop clock*, but because of its widespread use in schoolrooms in the late nineteenth and early twentieth centuries, it is now often called a *schoolhouse clock*.

Between 1850 and 1900 the United States produced, in addition to those particular clock styles we have noted, a great variety of clocks in diverse sizes, shapes, colors and materials. There are cases in the French style, cases with an Oriental flavor, cases of iron, papiermâché and marble, cases designed with Shaker simplicity and cases almost overwhelmed with Victorian fussiness. There are clocks with alarms that light candles and clocks with calendars that account for leap years. We close this chapter with a small sampling of products from the immense clock industry of nineteenth-century America (plates 47–52).

51.
Mahogany lamplighting alarm clock. The match was struck and the alcohol lamp automatically lit when the alarm rang on this brass-movement clock by the Ansonia Brass & Copper Company. American, Ansonia, Connecticut, 1869–78. Smithsonian Institution, National Museum of History and Technology, gift of the IBM Corporation

52.
Small papier-mâché shelf clock with mother-of-pearl inlay made by Chauncey Jerome. Jerome's papier-mâché clocks were popular in England as well as in the United States. American, New Haven, Connecticut, 1860–70. American Clock and Watch Museum, Bristol, Conn.

51

52

4 Clocks from Other Lands

The origins of American clockmaking can be characterized as the transfer of an art-technology from Europe to America. The origins of European clockmaking are much more difficult to identify. Recent studies in the evolution of the arts and sciences have changed the traditional view that the mechanical clock is a direct and deliberate technological improvement over the sundial, sandglass and clepsydra. A key discovery leading to the alteration of that view was made about 1900, when a fragment of a mechanical device was retrieved from a Greek ship wrecked near the Mediterranean island of Antikýthēra about 80 B.C. The device, known as the Antikýthēra Mechanism, was recently identified as a sophisticated astronomical model. It served no known useful purpose, but it was far from primitive—it even contained planetary gearing.

Two matters are now plain. First, geared mechanical devices of considerable complication existed centuries before the first mechanical clock appeared. Second, the building of these early devices was apparently not a response to a societal need but rather a demonstration of skill and of man's desire to show his ability to construct mechanical models of the world and sky. It is the growing realization that many instruments of science and technology developed *into* rather than *out of* their applications that has provided a new perspective on the origins of European horology.

Mechanical clocks first appeared in Europe in the late thirteenth century. By the seventeenth century distinctive national styles were developing, so that clocks from each area were taking on a character of their own. A brief survey will serve to contrast these styles and to illustrate some of the clocks that evolved within one country or another and that are of interest to collectors today—historically, mechanically, artistically.

Colorplate 13.
Renaissance-style astronomical table clock, unsigned. The exquisitely modeled case, in the form of an elaborate tower, is of gilt bronze and gilt brass and the dials are partly of silver. The large dial shows the time; the two smaller dials give astronomical information. German, probably Augsburg, early seventeenth century. Metropolitan Museum of Art, New York, gift of J. Pierpont Morgan, 1917

Renaissance Clocks   For convenience, mechanical clocks produced from the medieval period through the sixteenth century, whatever their national origin, will be considered under this heading. A distinction should be made, however, between the evolution of *public clocks* and that of *chamber clocks*. The former are large mechanisms intended for installation in a public location, most commonly a church. Chamber clocks are smaller devices for use in a room, or chamber.

All clockmaking activity to begin with depended on the invention of an escapement for releasing stored energy through the geared mechanism. The two predominant early forms were the balance wheel and the *foliot*—a crossbar with weighted arms that is attached to the verge and regulates the speed of the escape wheel; whether the balance wheel or the foliot came first is still in question. It was the appearance of practical escapements about 1300 that made both public and chamber clocks possible.

It should be borne in mind that through the fifteenth century clocks were only incidentally timekeepers. That is, rather than clocks as we think of them today, they were models of the universe incorporating a time-measuring function. Many early clocks, especially the public clocks, had no dial; the time-measuring function served only to cause bells to ring at scheduled times, to make moving figures dance at regular intervals or to operate objects representing heavenly bodies. Any clock that did have a dial had an hour hand only. There were two reasons for the absence of a minute hand. As already noted, these clocks were usually so inaccurate that anything more precise than an hour hand was hardly warranted, even though the trivial gearing necessary to incorporate a minute hand was well within the capabilities of clockmakers. Furthermore, these clocks were not being used to synchronize human activities, as clocks today do, so there was no particular need for accuracy. On the other hand, such dials as did appear on the early public and chamber clocks were often quite intricate, since astronomical and zodiacal information was frequently displayed along with the time (plate 53). In fact, some clocks used multiple dials to display the several aspects of the world model their makers had built into them and were, however unreliable as timekeepers, remarkably complicated mechanisms in other respects.

If any part of continental Europe can be thought of as the birthplace of Renaissance clockmaking, it would be the Augsburg area of Bavaria. This was the crossing point of medieval trade routes and in consequence the home of a variety of artisans and craftsmen renowned in many fields. Their skills in mechanics as well as in metalwork and other decorative arts, for instance, led them to create some of the finest clocks known. Their remarkable products were carried along the trade routes to other European centers and gave impetus to the rise of Renaissance clockmaking in Austria, France and Italy.

53.
Renaissance gilt-bronze astronomical table clock by Chasparus Bohemus, with designs after Hans Sebald Beham and Virgil Solis, two noted sixteenth-century Nuremberg artist-engravers. Besides giving the time, the dials provide calendrical and zodiacal information. Austrian, Vienna, 1568. Metropolitan Museum of Art, New York, gift of J. Pierpont Morgan, 1917

The cases of Renaissance chamber clocks, in Augsburg and elsewhere, were executed with much attention to decorative detail. They were most often made of metal, usually brass, and frequently fire-gilded. The mounts—that is, the supports or decorative appurtenances—were commonly gilt and represented birds or animals or more fanciful shapes. The Augsburg lion clock seen in plate 54, though dating from a later period, is a splendid example of Renaissance animal representation.

The cases were often finely engraved or pierced—piercing was customary on clocks with a strike or alarm since it allowed the sound to be heard more clearly. Scenes or patterns in high relief, called repoussé work, are not uncommon and are sometimes accompanied by enameling. Clocks of this period are occasionally housed in cases with such strong themes of their own—a case in the shape of a crucifix, for example—that the clocks themselves seem almost incidental.

55.
Iron Gothic chamber clock, with traces of gold leaf still visible. Typical features are the single-hand dial and the escapement controlled by a foliot, seen with its weights at the top. The dial appears to have been repainted. South European, c. 1500. Smithsonian Institution, National Museum of History and Technology

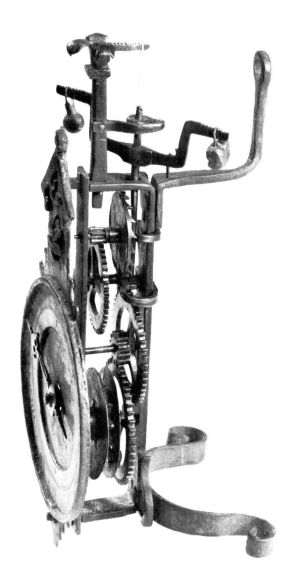

54.
Automaton lion clock. Standing on a base of ebony-veneered oak with gilt-brass mounts, the gilt-bronze lion blinks its eyes and opens its mouth as if to roar when the clock strikes. The movement, which may be seen through the glass apertures in the base, is signed *Christoph Miller (Müller?)*. German, Augsburg, 1643–50. Private collection

56.
A modern rendition in brass of Giovanni de Dondi's famous fourteenth-century astronomical clock. At top center is the dial of the Primum Mobile (a dial associated with medieval astronomy) and directly beneath it is the hour dial. Smithsonian Institution, National Museum of History and Technology

57.
Clock in plate 56: view showing the dial of Saturn (top center)

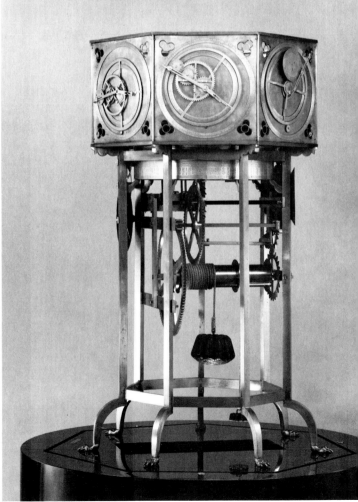

56   57

Chamber clocks became portable only after coiled springs had been adopted as a source of motive power. Exactly when this came about is uncertain, though there is evidence suggesting that it was no later than 1440. The introduction of the fusee, also in the fifteenth century, greatly improved the accuracy of the portable clock by eliminating the effect of the uneven torque supplied by the early crude spring.

Eventually, the timekeeping function of chamber clocks began to assume primary importance, and this led to the appearance of two new types. One was a simple weight-driven wall clock, often with no case at all and none of the traditional embellishments (plate 55). These have become known as Gothic clocks, even though most of them date from later than the generally accepted Gothic period (roughly, twelfth to sixteenth centuries). The other is a miniaturized clock, sometimes with a strike or alarm, small enough to be carried on the person; these have become known as watches and will be examined in the next chapter.

Public clocks developed concurrently with chamber clocks, although there are examples that antedate the earliest-known chamber clocks by about seventy-five years. As we have noted, they too were often mechanical marvels with elaborate astronomical displays and automatons—quite literally models of the heavens and the earth set to music and often embellished with dancing figures. By 1300 several escapement-controlled English church clocks were in operation; the earliest known, at Dunstable Priory in Bedfordshire, dates back at least to 1283. Richard of Wallingford, abbot of the Benedictine monastery at Saint Albans, in Hertfordshire, is credited with the design and initial construction in 1327 of an hour-striking astronomical clock that moved an astrolabe dial and displayed the motions of the sun, moon and (perhaps) the planets; it also incorporated mechanisms for showing phases and eclipses of the moon. Of several dozen other authenticated English church clocks built before 1500, special attention should be paid to the Salisbury Cathedral clock, which dates from 1386 and is the oldest surviving clock of the era. It may be seen in operation at the cathedral today.

Public clocks of this period were built on the Continent as well. The most famous and important of these is the astronomical clock by Giovanni de Dondi (1318–1389) of Padua, dating from 1364, which showed planetary motions, feast days, eclipses, the calendar and much more. De Dondi left a full set of sketches and descriptive material detailing not only the structure and operation of the clock but also how it could be reproduced. Several models of this masterpiece have been built in modern times from de Dondi's instructions; one of these can be seen at the Smithsonian Institution in Washington (plates 56 and 57). It is not possible for us to survey Renaissance public clocks in

58.
Iron model of the escapement and pendulum designed by Galileo more than three hundred years ago. This reproduction was constructed by L. C. Eichner in 1958 according to plans found among the papers of Galileo's son, Vincenzo. Smithsonian Institution, National Museum of History and Technology

59.
Bracket, or table, clock after the style of
Salomon Coster's first pendulum clock in
1657. This ebony-veneered example by
Johannes Tegelbergh has the time and strike
trains on one spring. Dutch, The Hague, c.
1670. Smithsonian Institution, National Museum of History and Technology, gift of
Dillard B. and Helen S. Lasseter

60.
Stoelklok with characteristic carved and
painted mermaids, gilt-lead cresting and
painted dial plate. Also characteristic are the
brass-clad weights and chains. Like most
Stoelkloks, this example is unsigned. Dutch,
Friesland, early nineteenth century. Private
collection

61.
Musical tall clock signed by Gerrit Van Der
Hey (at work c. 1750). Surmounting the
bombé case of burl walnut veneered on oak
and elm are gilt-wood figures of Father
Time, Mercury and Fame. The hand that
crosses the moon dial points to the title of
the tune being played on the musical attachment. Dutch, Amsterdam, mid-eighteenth
century. Metropolitan Museum of Art,
New York, gift of Mr. and Mrs. Herman
Pobliner, 1964

detail, but mention should be made of one famous surviving fourteenth-
century clock—the 1389 clock at Rouen, the earliest extant clock that
strikes the quarter hours.

To enter the seventeenth century is to leave the world of Renaissance horology. Clockmakers begin to concentrate on accurate timekeeping, with other functions secondary, and distinctive national styles
begin to emerge. But tradition dies hard, and the early years of the
seventeenth century still produced on occasion magnificent clocks in
the Renaissance spirit, sophisticated world models with beauty and
dignity—such as the German table clock shown in colorplate 13
(see page 64).

Dutch Clocks   Singular contributions to horology have come from
Holland, even though Dutch case styles as such have had little influence beyond Dutch borders. As we know, the earliest mechanical
clocks were regulated by the uncertain action of an oscillating wheel
or horizontal arm, not by a pendulum. In the late sixteenth century
the great Galileo had observed a swinging lamp in the cathedral at Pisa
and had then realized that a pendulum could be used to regulate a
timekeeper. Apparently, however, Galileo never solved the engineering problems involved, for, although an incomplete drawing of a
pendulum-controlled escapement was found in the effects of his son,
no model made by Galileo has ever been discovered. Moreover, models
subsequently made from his drawings (plate 58) have shown that his
escapement has basic technical flaws. In any event, it has never been
seriously applied to a clock.

It was the Dutch mathematician and scientist Christian Huygens
(1629–1695) who, around the middle of the seventeenth century, designed a workable escapement using the pendulum, and in 1657 a
bracket clock employing a modification of his design was made by
Salomon Coster (d. 1659) of The Hague. This clock had a short
pendulum and was housed in an ebony-veneered case; the dial was
sheet iron covered with black velvet and marked by means of a silver
chapter ring. The case style so introduced was used briefly by French
clockmakers before their own distinctive bracket clocks appeared
late in the century. Otherwise, except for a few examples made in
Holland (plate 59), Coster's clock had no progeny.

The importance of the pendulum as a regulator quickly became apparent, and clockmakers from elsewhere flocked to Holland to learn
how to use it. Among these were English clockmakers, and out of the
knowledge they acquired at The Hague and other Dutch centers was
born the great English school of clockmaking.

If the Dutch did not pursue their early lead in pendulum clocks,
they did produce a number of distinctive wall and tall clocks. One
type of wall clock from Friesland, first made about 1700, is the

60

61

62

62.
Unsigned *pendule religieuse* with red velvet dial surround. Tortoiseshell with brass inlay and gilt-brass mounts enliven the rather severe lines of this late seventeenth-century French pendulum clock. Private collection

63.
Unsigned Louis XV tall clock in a case of ebonized wood with brass mounts. A graceful circular mount surrounds the lenticle (small window) in the waist door, through which the pendulum bob can be seen. Northern French or Belgian, mid-eighteenth century. Private collection

63

Stoelklok, or "chair clock," so called because of the turned pieces resembling little stools which are set between the clock and its bracket, or shelf, and on which the clock sits (plate 60).

Dutch eighteenth-century tall clocks have certain features that tend to set them apart. Their cases, for example, are generally marked by a bombé section in the base and by finials in the form of mythical or human figures. A surprisingly large number of these clocks have a musical attachment that plays one tune or another on the hour, thanks to a multitune cylinder music box located within the case and above the movement (plate 61).

French Clocks French clocks—or, more exactly, the cases of French clocks—began to establish an identity of their own about 1660. French clock movements of the period are generally good but show little imagination. After the beginning of the reign of Louis XV (1715–1774), there were French clockmakers who did produce movements that still delight the enthusiast. But it is fair to say that many of the clocks made before the French Revolution (1789–99) are more notable for the cases in which they are housed than for the mechanisms inside.

The introduction of the pendulum-controlled escapement in Holland in 1657 was followed by a burst of activity among French clockmakers. Early French pendulum clocks were copied rather closely from early Dutch examples, though one known as the *pendule religieuse* is essentially French in case design (plate 62). The first true French styles were introduced toward the end of the seventeenth century, during the latter years of the long reign of Louis XIV (1643–1715). The most widely found style of this period is the bracket clock, a short pendulum clock typically 2 to 3 feet (61 to 91.4 centimeters) in height that stood on a matching bracket, or shelf, mounted on the wall. Since the somewhat delicate movements of these clocks could easily be damaged if moved inexpertly, case and mount were designed to encourage permanent positioning.

Both wooden and metal cases were made. The former, except for the earliest ones, are lavishly trimmed, with mounts of gilt bronze or silver as well as inlays of brass, silver or varicolored woods. Some dials are of engraved and gilded brass with each numeral in its own enamel plaque. Exotic materials such as tortoiseshell were often combined with engraving, piercing and sculpture to produce a striking effect. This style continued after Louis XIV's death, as we see in a superb example from the Régence period of 1715–23 (colorplate 14).

Tall clocks of the Louis XIV period are uncommon. More often one finds a bracket clock fitted to a separate matching pedestal that provides support just as a wall bracket would (colorplate 15). Such pedestal clocks superficially resemble tall clocks but are not in a single

Colorplate 14 (overleaf).
Bracket clock of the Régence period by Louis Mynuel (at work c. 1660–d. 1725). The case, attributed to Charles Cressent (1685–1768), a renowned French cabinetmaker also trained as a sculptor, is oak with tortoiseshell and brass marquetry and gilt-bronze mounts. Each hour numeral on the dial is in its own enamel plaque. French, Paris, 1719–23. Metropolitan Museum of Art, New York, Fletcher Fund, 1961

Colorplate 15 (overleaf).
Louis XIV pedestal clock by Jacques Thuret (at work 1694–d. 1738). The gilt-bronze-mounted case, attributed to André-Charles Boulle, the foremost cabinetmaker of his time, is oak veneered with tortoiseshell and white metal in the famous technique known as Boulle marquetry. French, Paris, c. 1700. Metropolitan Museum of Art, New York, Rogers Fund, 1958

Colorplate 14

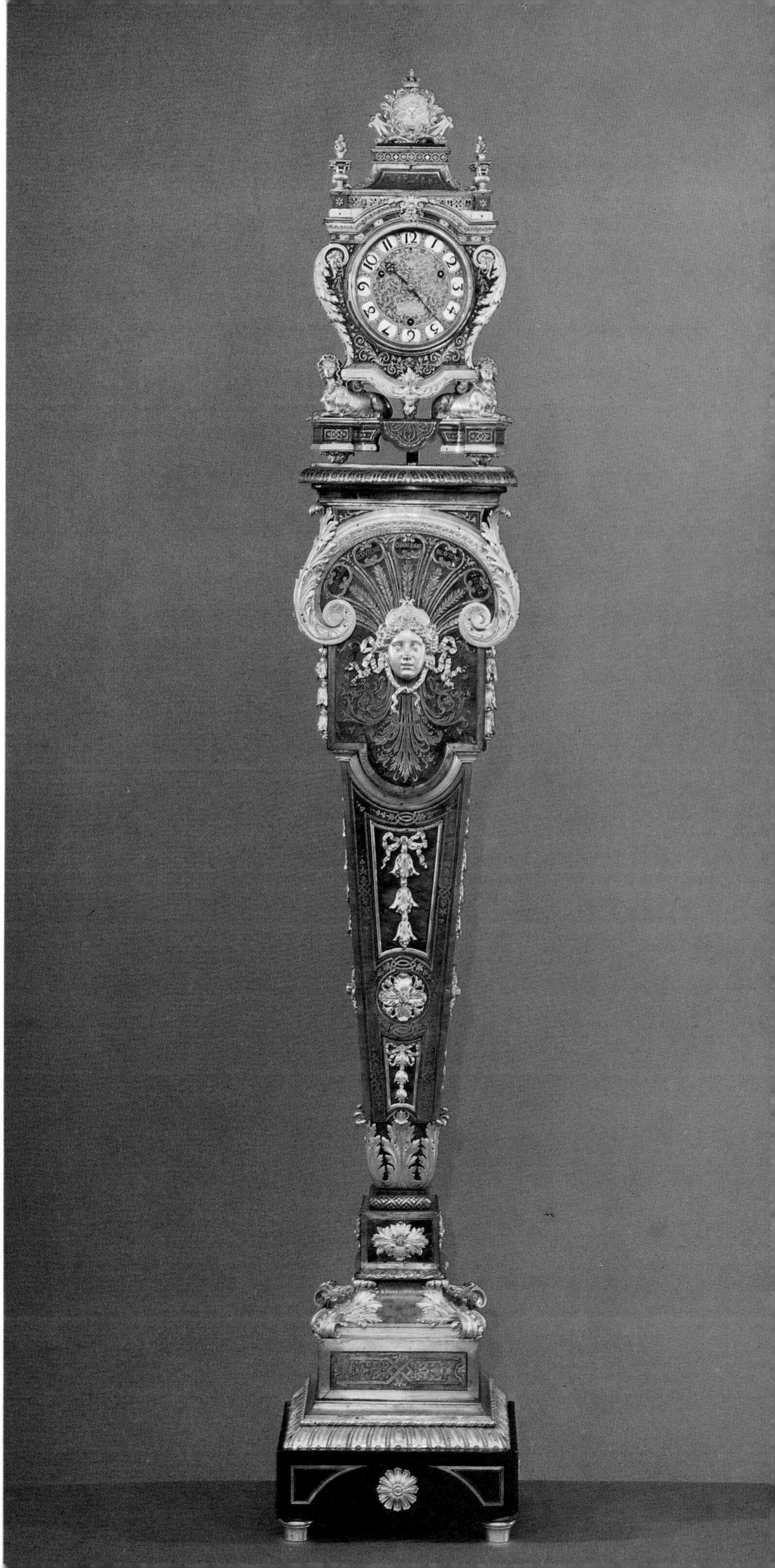

Colorplate 15

64.
Gilt-bronze and brass mantel clock in a late Louis XV design, with a movement by Jean-Baptiste Martre (b. 1734; at work 1770–85) and a rococo case signed *Dumont*. A music box is in the base. French, Bordeaux, c. 1775–85. Metropolitan Museum of Art, New York, gift of the Samuel H. Kress Foundation, 1958

tall case and lack a long pendulum. Designed to match the splendid clocks they support, the pedestals are ornamented with gilded mounts and elaborate marquetry veneering. One particularly notable type of marquetry introduced in this period adorned both clocks and furniture—namely, Boulle marquetry, a complicated technique using brass, pewter, tortoiseshell, mother-of-pearl, ebony and other materials, developed by the celebrated André-Charles Boulle (1642–1732), cabinetmaker to Louis XIV.

A greater variety of clock styles was produced during the reign of Louis XV than in any corresponding period of French history. A number of tall clocks, most of them made after 1750, can be found, though they bear little relationship to the important tall clocks that English makers began to build about 1660. Many of the eighteenth-century French tall clocks, in fact, are basically bracket clocks with hollow pedestals (the clocks having been refitted with long pendulums, the pedestals had to be hollow to accommodate them). True tall clocks often have a small window, or *lenticle*, in the waist at the height of the pendulum bob (plate 63). Pedestal clocks never have a lenticle. None of this is meant to imply, however, that Louis XV tall clocks are of no importance. Many are of much horological interest and are housed in cases of exceptional quality.

The cases of wall-bracket clocks of the Louis XV period are generally made of wood and heavily covered with decorative material, including colored horn and tortoiseshell, favorites also for use on tall clocks. Gilt mounts, gilt figures and other applied gilt decorations are standard. Dials now often have the twelve individual enamel plaques for the hour numerals surrounding a central enamel disk, with all thirteen pieces held in a gilt-brass frame; these are known as *thirteen-piece dials* and frequently are more ornamental than legible.

Several distinctive types of mantel clock appeared during the period. One employs grandly rococo cast-bronze cases (plate 64). Among the striking departures in design of these bronze mantel clocks is the abandonment of symmetry. Louis XIV clocks and early Louis XV clocks are symmetrical in overall design, although details of the applied gilt mounts sometimes are not. But this new breed of mantel clock generally ignored most aspects of symmetry, sometimes even in regard to the placement of the winding holes. The cast-bronze cases usually incorporated leaves, nymphs, flowers, shells and anything else that could contribute curved, flowing lines. The dials are nearly always one piece of enamel, with the numerals painted in black. The hands, in keeping with the case, are gilt and elaborately pierced.

Another type of mantel clock, often with the chinoiserie so typical of rococo decoration, has a small round case placed amid a profusion of figures, flowers and leaves of porcelain (plate 65). Again, symmetry

65

66

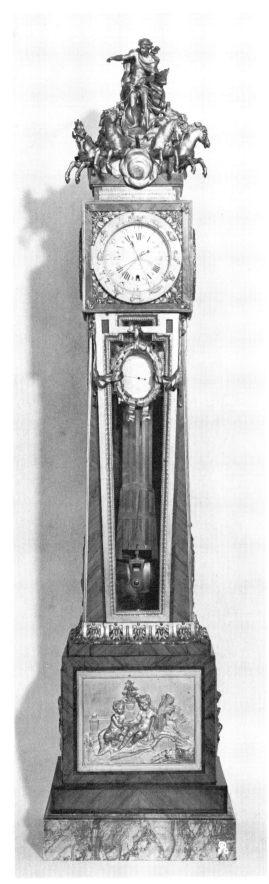

67

68

67.
Late Louis XV–period tall clock with calendar attachment. This sophisticated clock contains the work of three superb French craftsmen—the movement is by Ferdinand Berthoud; the case, of marble with tulipwood and kingwood veneer, is by Balthazar Lieutaud (d. 1780); and the gilt-bronze mounts are by the sculptor Philippe Caffiéri (1714–1774). French, Paris, 1767. Frick Collection, New York

68.
Louis XVI mantel clock by Jean-Baptiste Lepaute the Younger (1727–1802). The enamel ring dial of this white marble and gilt-bronze urn clock rotates, and the time is indicated by the bronze cherub's right

69

70

in both the supporting structure and the dial seems to have been deliberately abandoned.

Also popular during this period were wall clocks known as *cartel
clocks* (plate 66). These are housed in elaborate, generally asymmetrical cast-bronze cases that, like those of their cousins the bronze
mantel clocks, are built up with shells, figures and whatever else can
provide sinuous curves. A distinctive unifying principle of these
rococo decorations is the graceful C-scroll, a scroll carved in the shape
of the letter C, that appears again and again. Cartel clocks also have
one-piece enamel dials with painted numerals and elaborately pierced
hands. They range from about 1 foot (30.5 centimeters) to 3 or 4
feet (91.4 or 121.9 centimeters) in height.

Late in the Louis XV period French tall clocks began to be simpler
in design, with the abundance of curved lines giving way to fewer
lines and straighter ones. Furthermore, French clockmakers started
paying serious attention once more to the accuracy of their mechanisms. Julien Leroy (1686–1759) and his son Pierre (1717–1785) were
pioneers in this new generation of distinguished French clockmakers.
Another outstanding horologist of the time was Ferdinand Berthoud
(1727–1807), whose work reflected the growing influence of the

71.
Unsigned mantel clock of various marbles. French, late nineteenth century. Private collection

72.
Mantel clock of the Empire period in a case of blackened bronze with mounts of fire-gilt bronze attributed to Antoine-André Ravrio (1759–1814). The figure of a lady playing a musical instrument was a popular motif for Empire cases of this type. French, 1805–10. Cooper-Hewitt Museum, gift of the Estate of Carl M. Loeb

Colorplate 16.
Inclined-plane clock by Chartier made for
sale in the United States. (Note that the days
of the week are given in English.) It is
"wound" by putting it back at the top of
the plane once a week. The base is marble;
the clockcase, brass. French, Paris, c. 1900.
Private collection

73.
Morbier tall clock with a brass and iron movement and a painted wooden case. The round enamel dial with the pressed surround in lightweight brass is typical, as is the bulbous case. French, nineteenth century. Private collection

English school. Berthoud made precision tall clocks (plate 67) in cases substantially simpler than those of the earlier French rococo tall clocks, though even these are more heavily decorated than corresponding clocks in England.

The mantel clocks of Louis XVI's reign (1774–92) resembled those of the preceding years but with the introduction of neoclassical forms and decorative elements. Cases for some of these mantel clocks are still of bronze, but new case materials appear, notably marble (plates 68–70) and such other fine stones as alabaster. Alabaster was used particularly in conjunction with gilt statuary, and marble cases enjoyed a long period of popularity, extending well into the nineteenth century (plate 71). Cases of porcelain are also found, though less often, possibly because of their inherent fragility.

Mantel clocks in varying styles continued in vogue in Napoleon's day (plate 72) and throughout the rest of the nineteenth century. Cast-metal cases, both for mantel clocks and for the smaller boudoir clocks, persisted, and many of these became models for clocks in Victorian America (plate 50, see page 62). The period 1870–1900 was the only time in American clockmaking history that French styles had substantial influence. Even the heavy French marble cases, such as the one in plate 71, were imitated in America, as were the French cases of china and porcelain.

In reaction to extravagance in clock design, a trend toward simplicity on the part of a certain few clockmakers started in France about the time of the French Revolution and continued well into the nineteenth century (colorplate 16). A leading proponent of simple styles, styles almost austere when compared with those of most French clocks, was Abraham-Louis Breguet (1747–1823). Breguet is widely regarded as the greatest of all French horologists. He is known chiefly for his watches, though he did make a number of small clocks. A typical Breguet clock is housed in a rectangular case, largely devoid of decoration, and may have glass panels to reveal the mechanism. Its craftsmanship cannot fairly be called other than superb. Every piece bearing Breguet's name is a mechanical masterpiece. He is often imitated and forged, but very rarely has any of his imitators succeeded in duplicating the quality of his work. The story of French horology would be a proud one if it involved no one other than Abraham-Louis Breguet.

Certain French provincial regions produced styles of their own quite distinct from those of the Paris school, especially Breguet's. The most notable of these regions is in the Jura Mountains, along the French-Swiss border near Geneva. Clocks produced there have taken the name of Morbier, a district of the region; they are also sometimes called Comtoise clocks (plate 73). The earliest examples were made very late in the eighteenth century, and production continued until the time of World War I.

The movements of Morbier clocks are easily identified. They are constructed in an iron cage with horizontal top and bottom plates rather than the standard vertical plates. The striking is also unusual, as the hour is automatically restruck two minutes after the hour, often on a different bell or gong.

English Clocks   Prior to 1600 English clockmaking was largely confined to public clocks. About 1600 a weight-driven chamber clock began to appear. Known as a *lantern clock*, this was produced in England for more than a century, and modernized reproductions are made even today. Until the 1660s these clocks all had balance-wheel escapements (plate 74). Thereafter, lantern clocks with short pendulums called *bob pendulums* were made, and some with balance-wheel escapements were converted to pendulums, most of these conversions using the *long*, or *seconds, pendulum*, which takes two seconds to make a full swing and return (plate 75). The earliest lanterns had narrow chapter rings that scarcely projected beyond the sides of the clock. As the seventeenth century progressed, wider chapter rings that projected considerably farther became fashionable—thus providing us with a weak clue to the age of the clock. The basic design of the clock remained constant: brass side doors, brass dial with brass chapter ring (sometimes silvered), hour hand only (except on very late models or conversions), overhead bell, brass frets between bell and clock proper. Refinements such as quarter striking or musical attachments are occasionally found, but most lantern clocks are hour striking only and must be wound twice daily.

The first pendulum clocks to be made in England were probably the work of the Fromanteels, an English clockmaking family of Dutch descent. Only three months after Salomon Coster made his pendulum-controlled clock at The Hague in 1657, after the design of Christian Huygens, Ahasuerus Fromanteel sent his son, John (or Johannes), to Holland to work with Coster. John returned to England in 1658 and soon thereafter Ahasuerus offered for sale in London a clock with the new pendulum escapement. An early Fromanteel style was the architectural *hooded clock* (plate 76), clearly a forerunner of tall, or long-case, clocks. The first long-case clocks had short bob pendulums that swung directly behind the movement—the lower part of the case simply concealed the weights and supported the hood—and were generally less than 6 feet (182.9 centimeters) tall.

About 1670 the anchor, or recoil, escapement was invented, allowing the use of a much longer pendulum than the 6- or 7-inch (15.2- or 17.8-centimeter) bob pendulum. As a result, the 39-inch (99.1-

74.
Brass lantern clock with silvered chapter ring by Samuell Betts. Like all early versions, this example has a balance-wheel escapement and carries the hour hand only. English, London, 1640–50. Private collection

75.
Brass lantern clock by Thomas Loomes, with a movement that has been converted from balance wheel to long pendulum to improve its utility. The conversion was probably done in the seventeenth century, not long after the clock was made. English, London, 1659. Private collection

76.
Hooded wall clock of ebony-veneered oak by Ahasuerus Fromanteel. Its architectural design and narrow chapter ring indicate that it is an early model of this clock style. The triangular pediment and corner columns also appear on early English long-case clocks, of which this clock is an immediate ancestor. English, London, c. 1660. Metropolitan Museum of Art, New York, bequest of Irwin Untermyer, 1974

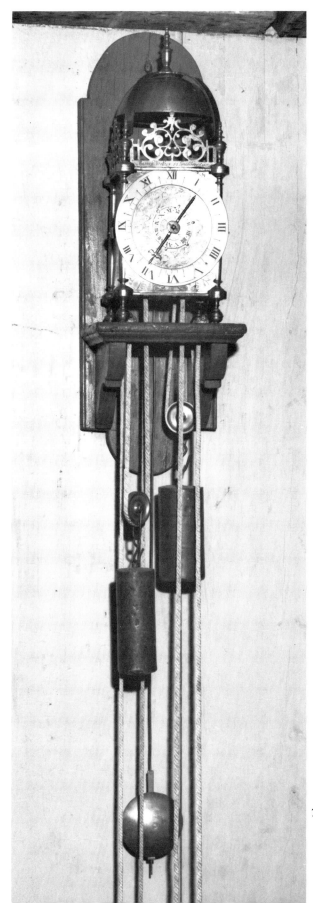

75

76

78

77

77.
Walnut-veneered oak long-case clock by Joseph Knibb (1640–1711). Its distinctive design features are the carved scroll crest and the spiral-turned hood pillars. English, London, late seventeenth century. Metropolitan Museum of Art, New York, bequest of Irwin Untermyer, 1974

78.
Clock in plate 77: detail of the gilded-silver and silvered-brass dial. Notable components are the exquisite hands, the calendar aperture and the three winding holes, which indicate a quarter-striking clock.

79.
Long-case clock by John Ashbrooke. A good example of floral marquetry is seen in the William and Mary case, which is walnut inlaid with various woods. English, London, c. 1700. Metropolitan Museum of Art, New York, gift of Alexander Smith Cochran, 1911

centimeter) seconds-beating pendulum was introduced and proved so superior to the short pendulum that it became known as the *royal pendulum*. (The earlier pendulum-controlled escapement required too large an arc of swing to allow a 39-inch pendulum to be practical.) Credit for the invention of the anchor escapement is usually given to the London clockmaker William Clement, although Robert Hooke (1635–1703), the famous English mathematician and scientist, also claimed the invention. In any event, the earliest surviving movement with an anchor escapement is Clement's and is dated 1671.

The next fifty years saw a maturing of long-case styles, the adoption of several important mechanical innovations and the achievement of a superlative level of craftsmanship. Indeed, the period from 1675 to 1725 is often called the Golden Age of English clockmaking.

An early change in long-case design was replacement of the triangular pediment of the architectural hood with a shallow carved crest; this was often accompanied by spiral-turned corner columns (plates 77 and 78). Later the carved crest gave way to a step-top hood—a sort of stepped pyramid with finials at the front corners and one on top. The step top became popular in America and is found on some American clocks as late as the Revolution.

Case decoration was both elaborate and superb. After the simple ebony veneer of the first architectural cases came styles of allover decoration of great artistic merit. Burl veneers were popular, as were several forms of inlay. Some of this inlay, in light-colored wood or even ivory, is fine-lined and intricate in pattern, and is called marquetry (plate 79). Japanning, simulated Oriental lacquer decoration, often with chinoiserie designs, became popular in the eighteenth century. (A contemporary American clock by Gawen Brown of Boston, in a japanned case, is shown in colorplate 8, page 32).

All seventeenth-century English long-case clocks have square brass dials with applied spandrels and chapter rings. The earliest dials are about 8 inches (20.3 centimeters) square, but by the turn of the century 11-inch (27.9-centimeter) dials were common. The arch-top dial so familiar today did not appear until early in the eighteenth century. Engraved and silvered brass continued to be the medium for dials until the last quarter of the eighteenth century, when the white-painted iron dial was introduced.

Of the great English Golden Age clockmakers, none was greater than Thomas Tompion (1639–1713), whose craftsmanship made him the premier clockmaker of his time (colorplates 17 and 18). Tompion, as did some of his contemporaries, made clocks that ran a month, three months, even a year on one winding. His clocks sometimes give the date, the equation of time (the difference between true and mean solar time), the phase of the moon and the time of high tide in London; the cases housing these masterworks are themselves artistic

Colorplate 17.
Superbly engraved backplate of the brass movement of the clock in colorplate 18. It is representative of the outstanding English workmanship of the time.

Colorplate 18.
Bracket clock by Thomas Tompion, often called the father of English clockmaking. The design of the gilt-brass-mounted ebony-veneered case is typical of the period. Also typical is the gilt-brass dial with silvered-brass chapter ring. English, London, c. 1700. Metropolitan Museum of Art, New York, gift of Irwin Untermyer, 1964

80.
Traveling clock with calendar and alarm, signed *Paulet* (probably Joseph Paulet). A repoussé case and champlevé dial distinguish this small silver and silver-gilt example, 9 inches (22.9 centimeters) high. English, London, c. 1700–1710. Metropolitan Museum of Art, New York, gift of Irwin Untermyer, 1964

81.
Brass-mounted ebony-veneered bracket clock by Christopher Gould. The four small corner dials are used to silence the strike (upper left), adjust the pendulum (upper right) and lock the pendulum (lower left and right). English, London, c. 1690. Private collection

achievements of the first magnitude—exquisite in design, medium, decoration and execution.

Occasionally one finds a unique clock from this era—for example, that shown in plate 80—but for the most part only three basic styles were made: the lantern clock and the long-case clock we have just discussed and the spring-driven bracket clock we noted briefly in Chapter 3. Spring-driven bracket clocks, as we saw, first appeared about 1670 and were designed for a bracket, shelf, mantel or table. The earliest were in rather plain, boxy cases, usually with a handle on top. Very shortly an ebony-veneered case was introduced, with brass mounts, a brass handle and a low basket top (plate 81 and see also colorplate 18). As the style evolved, the tops became more elaborate and were frequently decorated with gilt and pierced work. In the latter half of the eighteenth century they became simpler again, and the pierced work disappeared (colorplate 5, see page 29). Throughout the period of the traditional English bracket-clock manufacture, the sides and back of the case were normally fitted with glass panels, exposing the movement to view and thus displaying the workmanship of which the clockmaker was proud. The backplates of the movements, also easily visible, were often beautifully engraved (see colorplates 6 and 17).

The dials were always brass with applied chapter rings and spandrels. The earliest were square: arch-top dials were first seen shortly before 1720. The arch on a bracket clock is most often used for a decorative boss, a calendar dial (see colorplate 5) or a STRIKE/SILENT dial and less often for a moon-phase attachment. Styles of engraving, of hands and of spandrels tended to follow those for dials on long-case clocks.

About 1800 both long-case clocks and bracket clocks underwent major changes in style. The former, especially those made outside London, were often quite wide compared with the long-case clocks of a hundred years earlier. Moreover, by this time, as we have seen, the engraved and silvered brass dial was gone, replaced by the painted iron dial. Not even quality inlay work, craftsmanship on the movements and good case construction can disguise the fact that these wide, frequently clumsy cases are decorative failures (plate 82).

English nineteenth-century bracket clocks (plates 83 and 84) are smaller than their predecessors, much plainer and radically different from the traditional bracket-clock design. The number of distinct styles is large.

82

83

84.
Wooden balloon clock signed *William Lewis, London*. This is one of the many different types of bracket clock popular in England during the nineteenth century. English, London, c. 1810. Private collection

82.
White-dial long-case clock by John White-hurst (1713–1788) of Derby. The case, of mahogany with satinwood inlay, has the wider, flatter shape typical of the later English provincial long-case clocks. English, Derby, c. 1780. Metropolitan Museum of Art, New York, Rogers Fund, 1912

83.
Mantel, or shelf, clock signed *Brockbanks, London*. Clocks such as this inlaid mahogany and gilt-bronze example from the firm of John and Miles Brockbank were derived from the earlier bracket clocks. English, London, c. 1791–1806. Metropolitan Museum of Art, New York, bequest of Bernard M. Baruch, 1965

85

86

85.
Unsigned early nineteenth-century Japanese brass pyramid clock with a double foliot for day and night timekeeping. The wooden pyramid hides the clock weights. Private collection

86.
Japanese wooden pillar clock. This unsigned mid-nineteenth-century example strikes the hour; the strike movement is spring-driven and is part of the driving weight. Private collection

87.
Mid-nineteenth-century Japanese brass bracket, or table, clocks. The clock at left, in the walnut case, is a typical example of this type of clock. The clock at right has a double foliot and fixed dial rather than the more common balance wheel and adjustable dial. Metropolitan Museum of Art, New York, bequest of Thomas Egleston, 1900

Japanese Clocks   Mechanical clocks were unknown in Japan before European traders arrived in the sixteenth century. These traders, and the others who followed them until Japan closed its ports early in the seventeenth century, brought with them clocks as well as other Western goods. The Japanese copied the clocks, modifying them so as to accommodate their own timekeeping system.

The Japanese day was then divided into two periods—dawn to dusk and dusk to dawn. Each period was further divided into six equal parts, or "hours," the length of each hour varying according to the time of year. A daytime hour on a given day was equal neither to a nighttime hour of the same day nor to a daytime hour a fortnight away. Japanese clockmakers constructed their clocks so that they accommodated the variable hour. They also arranged a unique striking sequence. On the first of the six hours of one period, the clock struck nine; on the second hour, eight; finally, on the sixth hour, four. Strikes of one, two and three were reserved for use in temples. Scholars are still seeking a satisfactory explanation of why (by Western standards) the striking sequence is backward.

87

Most early Japanese mechanical clocks fall into one or the other of two categories: (1) *pyramid*, or *lantern*, *clocks*; (2) *pillar*, or *stick*, *clocks*. Japanese pyramid clocks resemble European chamber or English lantern clocks, but instead of standing on a wall bracket, they stand on a pyramidal base within which the weights descend and which, in turn, stands on the floor (plate 85). The escapement is controlled by a foliot instead of by the balance wheel normally found on early English lantern clocks. The movable foliot weights helped the Japanese adapt their clocks to their timekeeping system. Later pyramid clocks were equipped with two foliots, one above the other; control automatically shifted from one to the other at dawn and at dusk.

Pillar clocks are long and narrow, designed to be hung on a supporting pillar in the Japanese house (plate 86). The movement, at the top, is weight-driven and usually controlled by a *crown wheel* (a type of escape wheel), verge and balance wheel, although the balance wheel is occasionally replaced by a foliot or even a short pendulum. This type of clock has no dial. Instead, there is a pointer on the driving weight that reads on a scale attached to the lower part of the case. This scale has sliding indicators that are adjusted by hand to accommodate the variable hour length.

Early in the nineteenth century a portable spring-driven table clock, often called a bracket clock (plate 87), was introduced by Japanese clockmakers. It too was usually provided with an adjustable dial to suit the floating length of Japanese hours. This clock, generally regulated by a balance wheel, is much more "European" than the pyramid clocks or the pillar clocks.

In 1873 Japan adopted the Western system of timekeeping, and from then on the old-style Japanese clocks were no longer made.

Other European Clocks   After the introduction of the pendulum in Holland in the middle of the seventeenth century, clockmaking skills advanced in many European countries, and a variety of new local styles resulted. There are two we can single out as representative.

One is a charming style from the region of Sweden near the town of Mora (colorplate 19). The case of the clock is wood, and decorated in what can only be described as folk-art style. The round dial is painted on a metal plate; the brass hands are cast and hand finished. The movement, like most Swedish clock movements of the period, has iron instead of brass plates and is rather crudely made. It carries two bells and strikes in a dingdong fashion on the hour. (The common hour-strike system sounds three o'clock, for instance, by three successive blows on a bell. In the dingdong system three o'clock is sounded by three successive pairs of blows, the first blow of each pair on a bell of higher pitch than the second.)

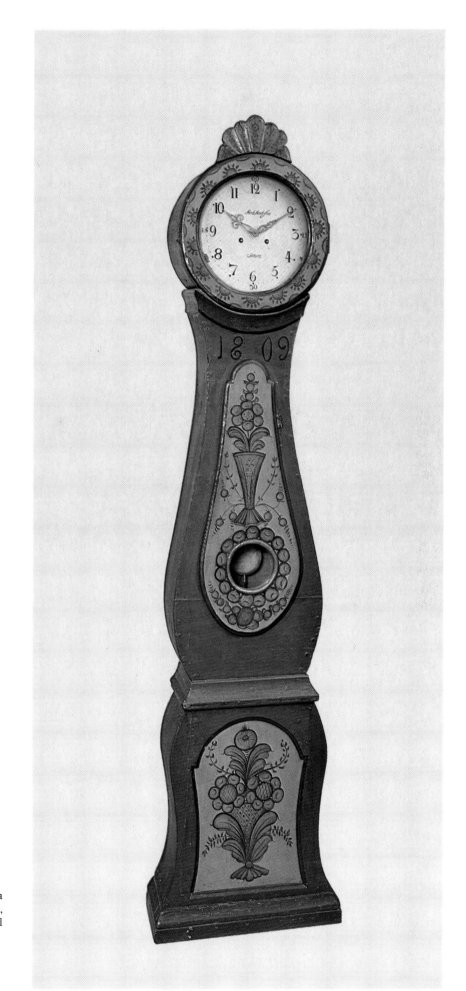

Colorplate 19.
Round-dial long-case clock from the Mora
region of Sweden. The painted wooden case,
which bears the date 1809, is a delightful
example of folk art. Private collection

The second of our two representative local clock styles is the important Austrian wall clock now known as the *Vienna regulator*. The earliest examples, which were probably inspired by contemporary English designs, appeared about 1780 and were housed in elegantly simple cases with some panels made of glass instead of wood. The hood was rectangular with a triangular pediment. The waist, or throat, was a bit narrower than the hood and had parallel sides. The base, also with parallel sides, contained the pendulum bob and was wider than the waist. The pendulum hung at the back and the weights descended in front of it, as was common in European pendulum clocks.

Gradually the cases changed, evolving through the styles of the Biedermeier period (1815–48) to become simpler and more severe. Often the differences in width between the case sections disappeared, leaving a case that was straight up-and-down (plate 88). After 1850 the straight lines of the late Biedermeier cases started to pick up ornamental carving, most often on the crest and the bottom bracket, although the half columns applied to the door also were frequently carved (plate 89). Finally, the cases made during the 1880s and 1890s, a full century after the clocks first appeared, were elaborately and heavily carved.

Movements of Vienna regulators are finely made, and commonly run for eight days, although there are examples, such as the one seen in plate 88, that run as long as six weeks on one winding. Some Vienna regulators are timepieces only; others are hour-striking clocks, quarter-striking clocks or quarter-striking *grande sonnerie* clocks (the quarter and the hour are struck each quarter hour). One noticeable characteristic of the Vienna regulator movement is that the pendulum makes an extremely short swing. Thus the clock can be accommodated in a quite narrow case.

88.
Vienna regulator signed *G. Mittag, Vienna*. This example, distinguished by its severely plain late Biedermeier wooden case, runs six weeks on a single winding. Austrian, Vienna, c. 1840. Private collection

89.
Unsigned quarter-striking wooden Vienna regulator with the ornamental carving common on this type of clock after 1850. Austrian, Vienna, late nineteenth century. Private collection

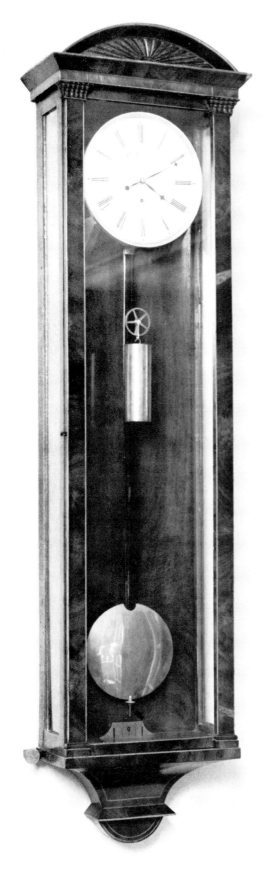

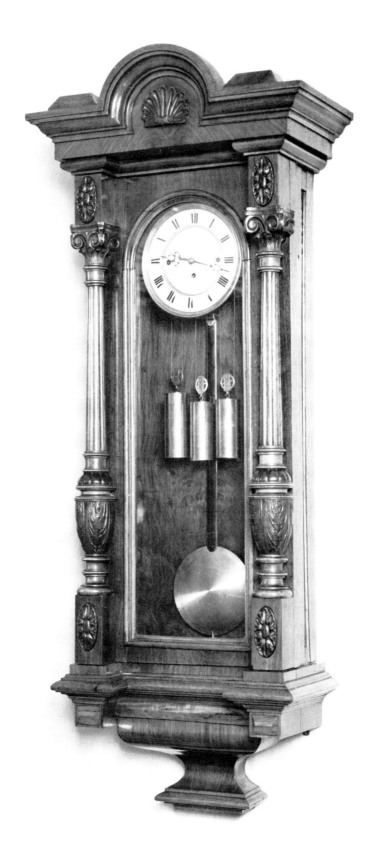

88

89

5 Time in a Pocket

A watch is a personal, portable timepiece; a clock, on the contrary, is normally fixed in place and not intended to be carried on the person. Before we begin our discussion of watches, however, we should understand some of the similarities—as well as the differences—between clocks and watches.

The source of energy for a mechanical watch is always a coiled spring. The escapement is always controlled by an oscillating member called the *balance*. Watches made after about 1675 have a wheel for the balance with attached *balance spring*, or *hairspring* (except of course for modern battery-operated quartz watches and such), but the connection between the balance wheel and the gear train varies. The time display on watch dials generally resembles the type seen on clocks, though a novel display is sometimes found. The running time of a mechanical watch is almost always one day (eight-day watches do turn up occasionally, however), whereas clocks have varying durations, depending on the designer's or maker's choice. For the mechanical connection in a watch a gear train is used, as in clocks. Watches made in the period when watchmaking had already become an industry are primarily timepieces only, in contrast to clocks from the same period, which usually include a second train that strikes the hours (sometimes the half hours and quarter hours, too). Watches made in the period when watchmaking was still a craft often include subsidiary trains that strike the hours, move tiny automatons, play music and so on. It should be realized, however, that these statements about adjunctive mechanisms are generalities: fine striking watches have been made in the modern industrial era, and simple timepieces were made in the sixteenth century.

The importance of a watch is judged in the same three categories as clocks—history, mechanics and artistry. Products of the American watch industry as well as European watches after 1850 are most likely to be noteworthy for their mechanical features and performance;

Colorplate 20.
Five magnificent enameled gold watches by five different seventeenth-century Parisian watchmakers: Goullons, c. 1650 (upper left); Nicolas Gribelin the Younger, c. 1680 (lower left); Christopher Morlière, c. 1650 (center); G. Gamod, c. 1640 (upper right); Auguste Bretoneau, c. 1650 (lower right). Metropolitan Museum of Art, New York, gift of J. Pierpont Morgan, 1917

90.
Ball-shaped Renaissance alarm watch in a three-footed gilt-brass case with pierced top and bottom covers. The iron movement with fusee is marked *Philipp Melanchthon*; the case is inscribed *Phil. Mela. Gott Alein. Die Ehr 1530*. German, early sixteenth century. Smithsonian Institution, National Museum of History and Technology, on loan from the Walters Art Gallery, Baltimore

90

91

watches made before 1675, for their decorative aspects and adjunctive mechanisms; watches of the intermediate period, for any or all of these.

We do not know when the first timepiece small enough and portable enough to be called a watch was built, or who built it. The German Peter Henlein (c. 1479–1542) of Nuremberg has been credited with the invention of a watch about 1500, but recent research suggests that small portable timepieces were already being made in the fifteenth century. Until about 1670, in any event, watches were a marvel of technology, often artistically interesting, but virtually worthless for telling time. They were, that is, ornamental and amusing rather than functional.

Some early watches are equipped with calendars and such astronomical indicators as moon phases or signs of the zodiac. Nevertheless, as with clocks of the period furnished with similar sophisticated mechanisms, these watches have only one hand—the hour hand. Although by today's standards the watches were poor timekeepers, they did serve a worthy purpose as well as exemplifying the remarkable skill of particular craftsmen, for in some contexts of the life of the period it may have been more important to anticipate a full moon than to know the time of day to the nearest minute.

Early watchmakers also often added such adjunctive mechanisms as striking parts or alarms (plates 90–92). A watch that automatically strikes the hours is called a *clock watch*; one that strikes only "on command," that is, when actuated by a pin or lever, is called a *repeater watch*. Clock watches and repeater watches are housed in cases pierced in many places to allow the bell sound to emerge; the pierced work is usually an element of the decorative plan of the case. Indeed, until the early seventeenth century, decoration on watches was mainly a matter of pierced and fire-gilt cases and engraved dials. In addition, since watches of the period lacked protective crystals or glasses, they were often fitted with a cover, pierced or solid, to safeguard the dial and hand. In the early 1600s the covers over the dials were often made of rock crystal; after about 1640 glass covers became common.

Two types of dial were popular in the seventeenth century. The *champlevé enamel dial*, introduced earlier, before the century began, was made by cutting grooves in the surface of a metal dial. The grooves would then be filled with colored enamels and fired (plates 93 and 94). Later in the century, after 1650, a dial was made in which the numerals were carved out of the metal dial plate and then filled with a black wax or black enamel, the rest of the plate being left unenameled. These latter dials are called simply *champlevé dials*.

Enamelwork on the outer surfaces of the cases was introduced in the early 1600s; the best-known school for this art form was in France, at Blois. (Five fine French enamel watches from Paris may be seen

91.
Watch in plate 90 with the outer cover opened. The studs behind each Roman hour numeral allow the watch to be read at night by touch; the small center dial is for setting the alarm.

92.
Renaissance clock watch with alarm, with its gilt-brass case opened to show the pierced work and engraving. The time train of the unmarked gilt movement has a fusee; the alarm and strike trains have stackfreeds. Probably German, c. 1570. Smithsonian Institution, National Museum of History and Technology, Munson-Williams-Proctor Collection

93.
Renaissance gold and champlevé enamel watch set in a little-finger ring. The watch-maker is Jakob Weiss of Augsburg, who became a master in 1584. German, Augsburg, c. 1584. Indianapolis Museum of Art, bequest of Ruth Allison Lilly

94.
Watch in plate 93 with the cover opened to reveal a tiny triptych depicting the Crucifixion and the symbols of Christ's Passion in champlevé enamel. The gold dial plate is also champlevé enameled.

93

92

94

95.
Cruciform watch in a tortoiseshell, silver and gilt-bronze case. The gilt movement with fusee is unmarked. Probably French, seventeenth century. Smithsonian Institution, National Museum of History and Technology, Munson-Williams-Proctor Collection

96.
Watch in plate 95 with the top and bottom covers opened to show the hinged panels of carved and pierced tortoiseshell

95

in colorplate 20.) Since the enamel cases were easily chipped or scratched, they required protection in use. This requirement probably led to the so-called *pair-case watch*, which had a separate and fully detachable outer case. It seems reasonable to suppose that Blois enamel cases were equipped with such protective outer cases, although none is known to have survived.

The pair-case style caught on, however, and was fashionable until the early 1800s. Indeed, many plain watches, such as the so-called puritan watches that appeared in England about 1640, normally came in pair cases, even though they had no delicate surfaces to protect. The pair-case fashion peaked in the late eighteenth century; English watches were then made with two or even three detachable outer cases. The outer cases themselves were usually decorated and sometimes covered with sturdy, wear-resistant material. Sharkskin held in place with an adhesive and with metal pins worked into a pattern (piqué work) was one decorative form. Leather and tortoiseshell were also used. Uncovered brass cases were commonly gilded and engraved.

96

97

98

97.
Silver skull watch. The gilt movement with fusee is unmarked. Probably French, eighteenth century. Smithsonian Institution, National Museum of History and Technology, Munson-Williams-Proctor Collection

98.
Watch in plate 97 with the jaws of the skull opened to show the dial. Note that the hands are missing.

99.
Watch in the form of an engraved and enameled gold beetle set with pearls and rubies. The watchmaker is unknown. Swiss, c. 1830–60. Indianapolis Museum of Art, bequest of Ruth Allison Lilly

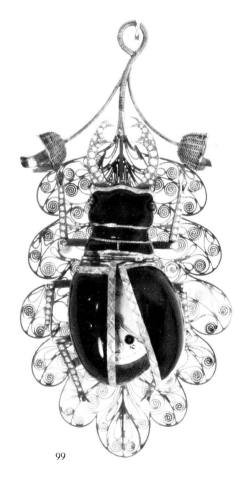

99

Watches mounted in fanciful cases—in the shape of skulls, flowers, crosses and such—had a period of popularity early in the seventeenth century (plates 95 and 96). Revivals of these *form watches*, as they were known, occurred in the eighteenth and nineteenth centuries (plates 97–99).

As has been noted, the escapement of early watches employed an oscillating member, or balance, superficially similar to the balance wheel seen on a modern watch. Initially, a horizontal arm with enlarged ends, looking somewhat like a dumbbell, was used, rather than a wheel. But whether wheel or dumbbell was used, there was nothing to supply a reliable restoring force to the oscillating member until the hairspring was introduced in the late seventeenth century. Many of the watches made before then were fitted with a straight-line, springlike piece that tended to urge reverse motion to the balance; this piece was usually a pig bristle, and the watches that had it are called *bristle watches*.

Finally, around 1675, about twenty years after he had designed his epochmaking pendulum escapement for clocks, the great Dutch mathematician and scientist Christian Huygens introduced the hairspring to the balance wheel of a watch. This was the first important

100.
Pair of chased and engraved gold open-face watches with *basse-taille* enameling. Made by William Ilbery for the Chinese market, they were decorated with an enamel painting in mirror image, a style popular with the Chinese. English, London, c. 1820. Indianapolis Museum of Art, bequest of Ruth Allison Lilly

engineering advancement in two centuries of watchmaking: it now became possible to produce watches with a timekeeping error of minutes per day instead of hours. The old crown wheel and verge escapement persisted, and would continue to be used well into the nineteenth century, but when equipped with a hairspring, it generally performed satisfactorily.

Until Huygens's hairspring, watchmakers tended to concentrate on the artistic aspects of their craft, paying special heed to the decoration of both case and movement. Once a watch could be turned into an efficient timekeeper, however, increased attention was given to the mechanism itself. The period from 1675 to about 1730 saw numerous advances in the mechanics of watchmaking.

In 1676 *rack striking* was invented by the Englishman Edward Barlow (1639–1719). This made possible the construction of repeater watches, which, as we have noted, are watches that will strike on command and perhaps indicate the most recent quarter hour, five-minute period, or even minute. Watches or clocks with rack striking will strike according to the particular position of the hour hand. (As pointed out earlier, the sequential striking in clocks is controlled by the simpler count-wheel, or locking-plate, system.)

The first new watch escapement, called the *cylinder escapement*, was perfected about 1725 by George Graham (1673–1751), nephew, last partner of and successor to the renowned Thomas Tompion. (When Tompion died in 1713, he was buried in Westminster Abbey, the first horologist to be so honored. When Graham died, Tompion's vault was opened, and Graham was buried with him. They are still the only horologists interred in Westminster Abbey. Their vault can be seen today, adjacent to David Livingstone's.) The cylinder escapement remained popular with Continental as well as English watchmakers well into the nineteenth century. A number of the magnificent watches from the workshops of Abraham-Louis Breguet, the great French horologist, are cylinder watches.

To work well, a watch escapement should have as little frictional contact with the balance as possible. Both the crown-wheel escapement and the later cylinder escapement had more frictional contact than is desirable. In 1759 an English watchmaker, Thomas Mudge (1715–1794), designed and built yet another escapement, called the *lever escapement*, and this did permit a large degree of detachment from the balance. For some reason, Mudge's invention was not enthusiastically received at first. Gradually, however, the merits of the lever became apparent, and after about 1850 it was standard for all watches, both in Europe and in America.

The champlevé dial continued to enjoy popularity in England for most of the eighteenth century. On the Continent, a white enamel dial with painted numerals had become popular, and this was eventu-

101.

Quarter-repeating automaton watch of chased and engraved gold with *basse-taille* enameling by an unknown watchmaker. The figures of Orpheus and Eurydice strike the bells when the repeating mechanism is activated. French, Paris, c. 1809–19. Indianapolis Museum of Art, bequest of Ruth Allison Lilly

102.

Chased, engraved and *basse-taille* enameled gold snuffbox decorated with pearls and an enamel floral painting and incorporating a double-dial watch and a music box. When the music plays, the cupids work at the forge. Swiss, c. 1825. Indianapolis Museum of Art, bequest of Ruth Allison Lilly

103.

Early twentieth-century gold complicated repeater watch, by the celebrated London firm of Dent, with a double split-second chronograph, a perpetual calendar with a hand to indicate the leap years and a minute-repeater mechanism. Smithsonian Institution, National Museum of History and Technology, on loan from the American Watchmakers Institute, Cincinnati

104.

Watch in plate 103 with the case opened to show the movement, which has a tourbillon escapement and is marked *Dent, Watchmaker to Her late Majesty*

ally taken up in England. It became standard on almost all watches throughout the nineteenth century.

Repoussé work came into fashion for the outer case about 1725 and remained in vogue for approximately twenty-five years. A popular metal for cases after its invention in 1720 was pinchbeck, an amalgam of zinc and copper resembling gold that was named for its inventor, the English clock- and watchmaker Christopher Pinchbeck (c. 1670–1732). Plain cases were sometimes covered with shagreen (sharkskin) or with imitations made of donkey- or horseskin and stained green.

Late in the eighteenth century a decorative style for metal cases called *engine turning*—the mechanical engraving of symmetrical patterns in curved, interlacing lines—became popular, especially on the Continent. This was likely due to the influence of Breguet, who favored elegantly simple decorative forms. Often used in conjunction with engine turning was *basse-taille*, a type of enameling that involves the application of translucent enamels on a metal base that has been patterned with engraving or engine turning (plates 100–102).

Much favored in the seventeenth century, enamelwork reached a new peak of popularity in the late 1700s and early 1800s (colorplates 21–26). It is often found on watch cases imaginatively shaped like flowers, insects or musical instruments (colorplate 27 and plate 99). It is also found on watches with automatons, three of which are shown in plates 101 and 102 and colorplate 28. The automaton watches of the early nineteenth century reflect a revival of the spirit of the medieval clockmaker, to whom a display of craftsmanship and artistry was of prime importance. Automaton watches are commonly repeater watches, and the figures visible through the dial of the watch begin to move when the repeating train is activated.

In the latter part of the eighteenth century, watches made on the Continent were generally thinner than those made in England. In fact, the persistence of the English watchmakers in continuing to produce comparatively thick watches helped to account for their fall from the position of supremacy they had held for a century. (Not all "thick" watches are undesirable, of course, as is demonstrated by the fine, relatively modern English *complicated watch* shown in plates 103 and 104.)

The adoption of Thomas Mudge's lever escapement made possible not only satisfactory timekeeping but also the production of thinner watches. The development of this kind of escapement, together with the trend to simpler decorative design, eventually led to the twentieth-century mechanical watch.

The nineteenth century saw the transition of watchmaking from a craft to an industry. Germany, England and France developed watch industries, though these were small compared with those of Switzerland and later the United States. The oldest Swiss watch factory, that

Colorplate 21.
Gold and enamel watch marked *Romilly à Paris* on a gold chatelaine decorated with pearls and enamel portraits of Louis XVI, Marie Antoinette and other members of the royal family and court. On the back of the watch itself is an enamel portrait of Marie Antoinette with her two children. Also suspended from the chatelaine are a royal seal and the key for winding and setting the watch. French, Paris, c. 1790

Colorplate 22.
Pair-case enamel watch with a gilt movement marked *Breguet à Paris, N. 17366*. Seen here is the back of the inner case, which is enameled with a portrait of a lady. The outer case (not shown) has a gilt frame with a glass back through which the portrait can be viewed. French, Paris, nineteenth century

Colorplate 23.
Back view of the elegant enamel case of a quarter-repeating watch. The gilt movement with cylinder escapement is marked *Breguet et fils, N. 2133*. French, nineteenth century

Colorplate 24.
Colorful enameled gold watch with scalloped edges viewed from the rear. The dust cover—the thin metal lid that protects the gilt movement—is marked *No. 47028, Breguet, Échap 'T. à Cylindre 4 trous en rubis*. French, nineteenth century

All four watches are from the Smithsonian Institution, National Museum of History and Technology, Munson-Williams-Proctor Collection

COLORPLATE 21

COLORPLATE 22

COLORPLATE 23

COLORPLATE 24

Colorplate 25.
Tear-shaped gold watch with an enamel
picture of fruit and flowers on the back of
the case. Its elaborately engraved gilt movement is marked *Ilbery, London 6142*. English,
London, c. 1780. Smithsonian Institution,
National Museum of History and Technology, Munson-Williams-Proctor Collection

Colorplate 26.
Watch in colorplate 25: front view showing
the dial, which is enameled with a scene of
two figures. The bezel—the metal ring that
holds the crystal—is set with pearls.

Colorplate 27 (above).
Enameled gold watch with a violin-shaped
case that opens to reveal the dial. The gilt
movement with fusee is marked *Carl Wurm
in Wien, No. 307.* Austrian, Vienna, nineteenth century. Smithsonian Institution, National Museum of History and Technology,
Munson-Williams-Proctor Collection

Colorplate 28 (right).
Chased and engraved gold automaton watch
displaying an enameled rural scene with
animated coopers working in the foreground.
Swiss, c. 1840. Indianapolis Museum of Art,
bequest of Ruth Allison Lilly

of Vacheron & Constantin, founded in 1785, introduced the principle of the interchangeability of parts to watchmaking in 1838, some two decades after the American clockmaker Eli Terry had introduced it to clockmaking. Another important Swiss watchmaking firm is that of Patek Philippe & Cie., founded by Antoine-Norbert de Patek in 1839. Adrien Philippe (1815–1894), who joined the firm in 1845, invented the stemwinding and stemsetting watch, for which he won a medal at the Paris Exposition of 1844. Earlier watches had been wound and set by the use of special watch keys.

A complete list of Swiss manufacturers would include many firms, some producing inexpensive wares, others watches of unusual shape with unusual dials (plate 105), still others high-grade precision watches, perhaps equipped with repeating mechanisms, perpetual calendars and even music boxes. Swiss complicated watches are highly desirable collectibles today. Simpler Swiss watches are also often worthy of a collector's attention, in spite of the vast number produced. By 1840 the Swiss had surpassed the English in watch manufacture; by 1870 they dominated the field. Switzerland exported 5 million watches in 1900 and more than 90 million between 1914 and 1919. In the single year 1974 the number of watches exported totaled 84.4 million.

American Watchmaking During its early years American watchmaking, in contrast to both American clockmaking and European watchmaking, had virtually no existence as a craft. Some early clockmakers made watches, but there are very few examples of their work extant today. Around 1810 Luther Goddard (1762–1842), a cousin

105.
Sector watch (so called because it is shaped like the sector of a circle) made by the Record Watch Company, Tremelan, Switzerland, in the late nineteenth century. Decorating the silver case is a tree and leaf design in Art Nouveau style. Each hand advances to the end of its scale and then "flies back" to the starting point. Smithsonian Institution, National Museum of History and Technology, Munson-Williams-Proctor Collection

106.
Luther Goddard's watchmaking shop in Shrewsbury, Massachusetts, about 1812. This artist's rendition was based on a description in *The Complete History of Watch and Clock Making in America*, by Charles S. Crossman, which was serialized in the *Jeweler's Circular and Horological Review*, 1885–87. Smithsonian Institution, National Museum of History and Technology

Colorplate 29.
The watch that launched the American watch industry—Howard, Davis & Dennison's eight-day pocket watch. This hand-some example, number 1 of about twenty gold models made for officials of Howard, Davis & Dennison, was presented to Edward Howard, founder of the company. Watch number 3 is known to have gone to David P. Davis, and it is assumed that number 2 went to Aaron Dennison. American, Boston, 1852. Smithsonian Institution, National Museum of History and Technology, on loan from the Massachusetts Charitable Mechanic Association, Boston

Colorplate 30.
Watch in colorplate 29 with the back of the case opened to show the gilt full-plate movement. The engraving reads *Howard, Davis & Dennison, Boston. No. 1. 8 day.*

COLORPLATE 29

COLORPLATE 30

of Simon Willard's, made a small number of watches at his shop in Shrewsbury, Massachusetts (plate 106). John D. Custer (1805–1872), a clockmaker of Norristown, Pennsylvania, was awarded a patent for a watch in 1843 and turned out a few examples, probably less than a dozen. Thomas Harland, of Connecticut clock fame, is said to have made watches in his Norwich shop before 1800 and hence may be America's first watchmaker, but only one authenticated Harland watch is now known.

Watchmaking as an industry in America began in a small way about 1840 and in earnest about ten years later, when Aaron Dennison (1812–1895) joined with the eminent Boston clockmaker Edward

107.
Pocket watch No. 9185 by E. Howard & Company. The initials *EKF* are on the front of the gold hunting case and the name *Arthur E. Edmonds* appears on the dust cover. American, Boston, mid-nineteenth century. Smithsonian Institution, National Museum of History and Technology, gift of Arthur E. Edmonds

108.
Watch made by the Hampden Watch Company under the ownership of John C. Dueber. The silver case is by the Philadelphia Watch Case Company. American, Canton, Ohio, c. 1890. Smithsonian Institution, National Museum of History and Technology, gift of W. Carl Wyatt Estate

109.
Watch in plate 108 with the back of the case removed to show the damascened nickel full-plate movement

Howard (1813–1904) and his partner David Porter Davis and started production of machine-made watches (colorplates 29 and 30). The firm of Howard, Davis & Dennison, later the Boston Watch Company, failed in 1857, but both the development of the American watch industry and the fortunes of Edward Howard were under way. In less than two years Howard formed a partnership with his cousin Albert Howard, and E. Howard & Company began the production of high-quality watches (plate 107). Under various names and changes of personnel, Howard's company remained in business even after he retired in 1882, and continued to manufacture his trademarked "Edward Howard" watches until 1903.

110.
Illinois Watch Company's Bunn Special in a gold open-face case. The notation above the seconds dial indicates that this railroad-quality watch has twenty-three jewels and runs sixty hours on one winding. American, Springfield, Illinois, c. 1910. Smithsonian Institution, National Museum of History and Technology, gift of W. Carl Wyatt Estate

111.
Watch in plate 110 with the back of the case removed to show the damascened nickel-finished movement with gold train and jewel settings

112.
Engraving of the watch factory of the Adams & Perry Manufacturing Company in Lancaster, Pennsylvania, 1875. Adams & Perry lasted less than two years, but from it sprang a series of companies that eventually culminated in the successful Hamilton Watch Company. Smithsonian Institution, National Museum of History and Technology

113.
America's first successful inexpensive watch—the brass-movement Waterbury "long wind" watch that sold for $3.50. This early example has a celluloid case; later examples had cases of nickel-plated brass. American, Waterbury, Connecticut, 1878. Smithsonian Institution, National Museum of History and Technology, gift of Meyer Browne

114.
Watch in plate 113 showing the dust cover with manufacturing data

From about 1860 on, a number of other watch-manufacturing enterprises were started. Many were unsuccessful, some going bankrupt even before any watches were produced. But a few were able to establish themselves, and soon the brands of watches that would become familiar to several generations of Americans began to appear. The American Watch Company—later known as the American Waltham Watch Company, later still as the Waltham Watch and Clock Company, and finally as the Waltham Watch Company—operated for almost a century, from 1859 to 1957, in Waltham, Massachusetts. The National Watch Company, founded in 1864, became the Elgin National Watch Company in 1874 and continued in business in Elgin, Illinois, until 1964. The New York Watch Company was organized in Providence, Rhode Island, in 1864, and underwent several reorganizations to emerge as the Hampden Watch Company of Springfield, Massachusetts, in 1877; in 1886 it was purchased by John C. Dueber, owner of the Dueber Watch Case Works, and operated independently in Canton, Ohio (plates 108 and 109), from 1888 until 1923, when a merger formed the Dueber-Hampden Watch Company. In 1927, two years after it had been sold for more than a million dollars, the company went into receivership, and in 1930 its equipment was sold to the Soviet Government, which was in the process of establishing a watch factory in Moscow.

The Illinois Springfield Watch Company, of Springfield, Illinois, made its first watches in 1872 and continued manufacturing until 1933, although in 1885 its name was changed to the Illinois Watch Company (plates 110 and 111) and in 1928 it was sold to the Hamilton Watch Company. The Hamilton Watch Company itself began production in 1893 in Lancaster, Pennsylvania, but the company had already undergone various reorganizations and name changes, having started as the Adams & Perry Manufacturing Company of Lancaster in 1874 (plate 112). The Seth Thomas Clock Company is noteworthy for being the only clock company to produce high-grade watches; this it did from 1884 to 1915.

The objective of all these companies, and of others too, was to manufacture handsome, reliable timekeepers for a highly competitive market. During the late 1880s sporadic efforts were made to establish uniform performance standards for watches used on railroads, but not until after a disastrous wreck in 1891 on the Lake Shore and Michigan Southern Railroad, a wreck blamed on a timekeeping error, were the efforts successful. It then became common practice to refer to reliable American pocket watches as railroad watches, although to be certified as such, watches had to meet the exacting railroad standards in repeated tests. So adept did Americans become at producing watches of high performance standards that certain Swiss manufacturers began making watches closely imitating their American counterparts.

Howard, Illinois, Elgin and other American watches, while priced to attract a range of buyers, could not reasonably be called inexpensive watches. In the 1870s, however, the attention of the watch industry began to turn to the design and manufacture of a truly low-priced, mass-market watch. After a few failures, a watch designed by Daniel A. A. Buck of Waterbury, Connecticut, and manufactured by the Benedict & Burnham Manufacturing Company of Waterbury, was introduced in 1878. This watch (plates 113 and 114), selling for $3.50, was so successful that the Waterbury Watch Company was formed in 1880 to manufacture it. The company continued to do so until 1891. The movement of this bargain watch is fascinating to observe, and observation is easy, for early models had a skeletonized dial (a dial in which the center part is cut away) and a skeletonized movement as well. The minute hand is attached to the frame of the movement, and the movement itself turns in the case once an hour (in the more conventional movement, the minute hand is attached to a gear and the gear makes the hourly revolution). The gearing needed to drive the hour hand at the rate of one revolution in twelve hours had been designed much earlier—by James Ferguson (1710–1776), a Scottish astronomer and mathematician. The spring of the Waterbury watch is 9 feet (274.3 centimeters) long, and it takes 150 half turns of the stem before the watch is fully wound. Because of this characteristic, the watch was nicknamed the "long wind" and Waterbury was sometimes called the "land of eternal spring."

The quest for low-priced watches was carried further by the Ingersoll brothers, Robert Hawley (1859–1928) and Charles Henry (1865–1948), who commissioned the Waterbury Clock Company (not the Waterbury Watch Company) to make a watch to sell cheaply at the World's Columbian Exposition in Chicago in 1893 (plate 115). The watch sold well, and in 1896 the Ingersolls introduced their Yankee model, "The Watch That Made the Dollar Famous," as their slogan had it. The Yankee did indeed sell for one dollar, and Ingersoll watches were henceforth called dollar watches.

The cases of the earliest American watches were either of silver or of eighteen- or fourteen-karat gold, often handsomely engraved, engine-turned or inlaid with multicolored golds. Both hunting-case models—models with a metal cover over the face released by pressing the stem—and open-face models were popular. Collectors will find that sometimes gold cases have been claimed for their metal value and the original watch movements rehoused in lesser cases. Rehousing is easiest to spot when a different type of case has been substituted. Open-face watches always have the winding stem at 12; hunting-case watches always have the winding stem at 3. Lower-quality cases were gold-filled, gold-plated or nickel-plated. As we have seen, the original Waterbury case was of lower quality yet, being made of celluloid.

115.
Pocket watch commissioned from the Waterbury Clock Company by R. H. Ingersoll & Brother, New York, for sale at the World's Columbian Exposition in Chicago. The back of the gold-plated brass case bears designs honoring Christopher Columbus. American, Waterbury, Connecticut, 1893. Smithsonian Institution, National Museum of History and Technology, gift of George R. Hyde

6   Advice for Collectors

Knowledge and purpose are to a collector what intuition and impulse are to an accumulator. With knowledge comes purpose, and with purpose comes discrimination. Acquiring information is therefore the first step in acquiring a superior collection. Would-be collectors can prepare themselves by reading, looking and listening. There are many good books on clocks and watches, and outstanding clock and watch collections may be seen in a number of museums. Listening to experienced collectors who enjoy sharing their expertise and interests is highly rewarding for beginners, and membership in a collectors' group, such as the National Association of Watch and Clock Collectors, whose headquarters are in Columbia, Pennsylvania, can provide introductions to many such collectors. Through study and contact with collections and collectors, beginners will learn not only how to recognize a particular timepiece but also why it is worth looking at. They will discover, too, where their main interests lie and will then be ready to choose a focus for their own collections.

Purposeful collectors should ask two questions of every potential acquisition: Would this type of timepiece enrich my collection as now planned? Is this particular example fit to be added to my collection? Only when the answer to both questions is yes should the collector seriously consider buying the piece.

As an illustration, let us imagine that a collector of Pennsylvania tall clocks has an opportunity to buy a flat-top tall clock signed *George Hoff, Lancaster*. Historically, the piece would represent the superior Lancaster County clockmaking of the last third of the eighteenth century. Mechanically, it would represent the German type of movement, with the distinctive open-ended lantern pinions that are far more reliable than they seem. Artistically, it would represent a style popular on early, simple clocks and rarely seen after 1800. Armed with this information about the clock's history, mechanics and position as a piece of decorative art, the collector can decide whether the piece would truly have a place in the scheme of the collection.

Let us assume that the clock would indeed be an appropriate acquisition. Now the collector must determine if it is worth buying. Three aspects must be examined: integrity, condition and appearance. Integrity is another word for authenticity: Is the clock a real George Hoff, or is it a fake—a mélange of old and new parts being passed off as an original? Because skilled but unscrupulous craftsmen do exist and because only an expert is likely to spot a counterfeit, collectors, especially beginners, should trade only with established dealers or reputable private collectors.

As for the condition of our hypothetical George Hoff flat top, it should be such that the clock can be added directly to the collection without extensive restoration. This means that the movement should be in good running order—cleaned, oiled and adjusted, and repaired where necessary. The case should be structurally sound, and all restorations, if any, clearly and fully documented. Realistically speaking, very few clocks survive as much as two hundred years of changing ownership, not to mention adverse environments, neglect and even abuse, without sustaining some damage or deterioration. Collectors often must choose between a clock that has been restored and one in which structural parts are missing. For most collectors, the restored piece will be the better choice, but only if the restoration has been done by someone skilled in the methods, materials and designs appropriate to the clock—in other words, done as if directed by the maker. Collectors who decide to buy "in the rough" and do the restoration themselves must be prepared to invest a great deal of time, money and effort in getting their timepieces back in working order.

Judging the appearance of the clock calls for taste and some knowledge of the decorative arts. To want to add a flat-top tall clock to a collection is one thing; to know whether the flat top under consideration is a superior example or something much less is quite another. Sometimes a collector who is aware that a clock is inferior will buy it in the hope of "trading up" at a later date, but it is generally better to start with a good example, especially in the beginning stages of a collection.

To all collectors, novice or expert, no matter what their specialty, one final bit of advice about the timepieces already in their collections: enjoy them. Listen to them and let them be a part of the family. Think of the history that unfolded around them. Marvel that generations long gone heard their sounds just as we hear them today. Each piece has its own voice and personality, its own special way of stirring a memory or an emotion. To plan and assemble a collection is a task for the mind, but to live with it is a joy for the spirit.

Glossary

arbor, an axle or shaft.

automaton clock or watch, a timekeeper with animated figures activated by the mechanism of the clock or watch.

balance spring, see *hairspring*.

balance wheel, a wheel or ring that oscillates about its own axis and synchronizes the running rate of a clock or watch with its natural frequency of oscillation; also called a balance.

banjo clock, any wall clock or timepiece derived from Simon Willard's "Improved Timepiece" of 1802. The name presumably came from the resemblance of Willard's clock to a banjo.

base, the lowest of the three sections of a tall-clock case; also called the *plinth*.

basse-taille, an enameling technique used on engraved or engine-turned watch dials and cases.

bonnet, see *hood*.

boss, a rounded protruding ornament attached to the dial or case of a clock; on the dial, commonly carries the maker's identification.

bracket clock, originally a seventeenth- or eighteenth-century clock intended to stand on a matching wall bracket.

cartel clock, a French wall clock of the Louis XV period; usually in an asymmetrical cast-bronze case heavily decorated with curving rococo designs.

chamber clock, a mechanical timepiece made small enough for use in a room, or chamber, as opposed to a *public clock*; generally refers to timepieces made before the seventeenth century.

champlevé dial, a type of dial introduced in the seventeenth century. The numerals on a metal dial are hollowed out below the level of the dial plate and then filled with black wax or black enamel.

champlevé enamel dial, a type of dial introduced at the end of the sixteenth century. Grooves are cut in a metal dial plate, filled with colored enamels and fired, contriving floral designs, religious scenes and other pictorial decoration.

chapter ring, the annular part of a clock dial containing all the markings associated with the minute and hour hands.

chimney, the supporting base, or *plinth*, of a *finial*.

clock watch, a watch that strikes the hours or quarter hours automatically.

complicated clock or watch, a clock or watch with more adjunctive mechanisms than are usually encountered.

count wheel, an irregularly notched wheel that controls the number of blows given by the *striking hammer* when it sounds the time; also called a locking plate. A clock with this type of strike control strikes the hours sequentially. See plate 10.

crown wheel, an early type of *escape wheel* used in conjunction with the *verge* in both clocks and watches. Its teeth stand perpendicular to its plane, giving it a crownlike appearance.

crutch wire, a wire or rod, attached to the *verge arbor*, that transmits the power from the escape wheel to the pendulum. See plate 10.

drum, the thick section of the *arbor* of a weight-driven clock around which the weight cord is wrapped when the clock is wound. See plate 9.

dust cover, a thin protective metal lid fitted over the movement of a watch.

escapement, a device that controls the energy driving the mechanism of a clock or watch and determines the rate of timekeeping. Its basic components are an *escape wheel*, a *verge* and a *pendulum* or a *balance*. Anchor or recoil, a clock escapement invented about 1670, probably by William Clement, in which the *escape wheel* reverses direction slightly (recoils) after each interception by the *verge*. Crown wheel and verge, the oldest type of clock and watch escapement known. Cylinder, a watch escapement perfected by George Graham about 1725; it is not used today. Deadbeat, a clock escapement invented about 1715 by George Graham; more generally, any clock or watch escapement with no recoil. Lever, a watch escapement invented by Thomas Mudge in 1759; now standard on all mechanical watches. Pinwheel, a clock escapement in which the *escape wheel* is not toothed but has "pins" projecting from one side. Tourbillon, a rotating watch escapement invented to eliminate position errors.

escape wheel, the last wheel of the *time train* of a clock or watch; the wheel through which the driving force is released for delivery to the *pendulum* or the *balance wheel*. See plate 10.

fan-fly or *fly*, a flat piece of material mounted on the final *arbor* of the *strike* (or chime) *train*; regulates the speed of the train. See plate 11.

finial, a turned, carved or molded ornament, generally of brass or wood; usually mounted at or near the top of a clock-case.

fire gilding, a method of gilding metal. An amalgam of gold and mercury is applied to the metal, which is then heat treated to vaporize the mercury, leaving a thin film of gold that will later be burnished.

foliot, a horizontal, end-weighted rod, attached to a *verge*, that oscillates in a horizontal plane and is the rate controller for some early European and Japanese clocks. The speed of its oscillation is regulated by moving its weights—the nearer they are to the center, the faster the oscillation. See plate 55.

form watch, a watch whose case is in the form of an object unrelated to horology —a skull, for example, or a violin.

fusee, a spirally wound conical pulley used in spring-driven clocks and watches to make the driving force of the *main-spring* uniform over the full running period. See plate 39.

gallery clock, a timepiece, usually made to be readable at a distance; often mounted on the face of the gallery in an assembly hall so the speaker can see it.

gear train, a complete, intermeshed set of *wheels* and *pinions* linking an energy source to the performance of a specific function. Thus, the *time train*, or *going train*, leads to the registry of time; the *strike train* to the striking of the hours; the *chime train* to the sounding of simple tunes to denote other time points, such as quarter hours. See plates 9 and 10.

hairspring, a thin spiral spring attached to a *balance wheel* to regulate its motion; also called a balance spring.

hood or *bonnet*, the upper section of a tall-clock case, housing the dial and movement.

hunting-case watch, a watch whose dial glass is covered by a metal lid or cover that flies open when the winding stem is pressed.

lantern clock, a seventeenth- or early eighteenth-century wall-mounted weight-driven clock; primarily English.

leaves, the teeth of a *pinion*.

lenticle, a small window in the *waist* door of a tall clock positioned at the level of the *pendulum bob* so that the pendulum's motion can be seen.

locking plate, see *count wheel*.

mainspring, the coiled spring that provides the motive power for spring-driven clocks and watches.

moon dial, a dial showing the phases of the moon; often found in the arch of a clock dial.

motion work or *motion train*, the *gear train* that provides twelve-to-one speed reduction so that a minute hand and an hour hand can be driven simultaneously.

open-face watch, a watch with no cover over its dial glass, as opposed to a *hunting-case watch*.

pair-case watch, a watch with a complete and removable outer case into which the inner case containing the movement is fitted.

pendulum, a vertical rod, usually with a weight called a bob at its lower end; oscillates in a vertical plane when suspended from a fixed point. In a pendulum clock, the natural frequency of the pendulum's swing controls the clock's running rate. *Bob pendulum*, a short pendulum, 6 or 7 inches (15.2 or 17.8 cm.) long; beats half seconds or less; usually has a relatively wide arc of swing. *Seconds, seconds-beating* or *long pendulum*, 39.14 inches (99.4 cm.) long; beats once a second, thus requiring two seconds to make a full swing and return; also called a royal pendulum.

pillar, a wood or metal piece attached to the *plates* of a clock or watch to hold them rigidly in position. See plate 9.

pinion, a small toothed wheel (gear) in a *gear train*; typically has six to ten teeth called leaves. *Cut pinion*, one whose leaves are cut from solid stock. *Lantern pinion*, one whose leaves are individual small rods, or wires, affixed in a circle between two disks and spaced so that they engage the teeth of a wheel. *Roller pinion*, same as the lantern, except that the wires forming the leaves are sheathed in loose sleeves of metal or wood.

pivot, the pin in each end of an *arbor*.

plates, two parallel flat sheets of metal or wood which are held separate by *pillars* and between which the *gear trains* of a clock or watch are fitted. See plates 9 and 11.

plinth, the base, or lowest section, of a tall-clock case. Also, the block supporting a *finial*; in this case, often called a *chimney*.

public clock, any large clock intended for service in or on a public building in a location where it can be viewed by many people, perhaps from a considerable distance.

rack striking, a system for controlling the *strike train* so that the number struck is determined by the position of the hour hand rather than by the number previously struck, as with *count-wheel striking*.

repeater watch, a watch that, by depressing a pin or moving a lever on it, can be activated to strike a specified time point. An *hour repeater* gives the hour just past; a *quarter repeater*, the quarter; a *minute repeater*, the minute. Repeater mechanisms are also found on clocks.

repoussé work, decoration in high relief on metal, hammered or punched up from the underside; used on watch- and clockcases, especially in the seventeenth and eighteenth centuries.

spandrel, a cast-metal cornerpiece or an engraved or painted design decorating the corner areas of a clock dial; also, the area where such decoration is found.

splat, a painted, veneered or carved panel placed at the top of many clocks.

spring barrel, a cylinder containing the coiled *mainspring* of a spring-driven clock or watch. The first wheel of the *gear train* forms one end of the cylinder.

stackfreed, an early device used to equalize the driving force of a *mainspring*; supplanted by the *fusee*.

strike train, see *gear train*.

striking hammer, a weighted rod, activated by the *strike train*, that hits a bell or gong and thus sounds a given time. See plate 8.

suspension, the means by which a pendulum is hung. *Suspension spring*, the spring—a flat, flexible part at the top of a pendulum—by which the pendulum is suspended. *Trapeze suspension*, a method of suspending a pendulum by hooking it over a U-shaped cord or wire that swings like a trapeze.

tablet, a reverse-painted, stenciled, etched or transfer-printed glass panel decorating many nineteenth-century American wall and shelf clocks.

throat, the narrow center section of certain wall clocks, especially the banjo clock and the Vienna regulator.

time train or *going train*, see *gear train*.

trunk, see *waist*.

verge, in early clocks and watches, a rod carrying two pallets (projections, or lips) that intercept the motion of the *crown wheel;* also, the *arbor* for the *balance wheel* or the *foliot.* In later clocks and watches, more generally the device that intercepts the motion of the *escape wheel.* See plate 10.

wagon-spring clock, any of several types

of clock powered by flat, iron leaf springs (similar to those used in wagons) instead of coiled springs. The flat springs are drawn into a bent position when the clock is wound, and the energy they expend in returning to their original flat shape is enough to run the clock. At first called the accelerating lever spring

clock by its inventor, Joseph Ives.

waist or *trunk,* the central section of a tall-clock case.
wheel, a toothed gear in a *gear train.*
white dial, a tall-clock dial of white-painted iron; superseded the engraved brass dial in both England and America after about 1780.

Reading and Reference

General
BRITTEN, F. J. *Britten's Old Clocks and Watches and Their Makers.* 8th ed., by Cecil Clutton and the late G. H. Baillie and C. A. Ilbert, rev. and enl. by Cecil Clutton. New York: E. P. Dutton and Co., 1973.
CHAMBERLAIN, PAUL M. *It's About Time.* 1941. Reprint. London: Holland Press, 1964.
CLUTTON, CECIL, AND GEORGE DANIELS. *Watches.* New York: Viking Press, 1965.
DANIELS, GEORGE. *English and American Watches.* New York: Abelard-Schuman, 1967.
LLOYD, H. ALAN. *The Collector's Dictionary of Clocks.* London: Country Life, 1964.
RAWLINGS, A. L. *The Science of Clocks and Watches.* 2d ed. 1948. Reprint. Wakefield, Yorkshire, England: E. P. Publishing Ltd., 1974.

ROBERTSON, J. DRUMMOND. *The Evolution of Clockwork.* 1931. Reprint. Wakefield, Yorkshire, England: E. P. Publishing Ltd., 1972.

American Clocks and Watches
BAILEY, CHRIS H. *Two Hundred Years of American Clocks and Watches.* Englewood Cliffs, N.J.: Prentice-Hall, 1975.
BATTISON, EDWIN A., AND PATRICIA E. KANE. *The American Clock, 1725–1865.* Greenwich, Conn.: New York Graphic Society, 1973.
DISTIN, WILLIAM H., AND ROBERT BISHOP. *The American Clock.* New York: E. P. Dutton and Co., 1976.
PALMER, BROOKS. *The Book of American Clocks.* New York: Macmillan Co., 1950.
PALMER, BROOKS. *A Treasury of American Clocks.* 2d ed. New York: Macmillan Co., 1967.

ROBERTS, KENNETH D. *Contributions of Joseph Ives to Connecticut Clock Technology, 1810–1862.* Bristol, Conn.: American Clock and Watch Museum, 1970.
ROBERTS, KENNETH D. *Eli Terry and the Connecticut Shelf Clock.* Bristol, Conn.: Ken Roberts Publishing Co., 1973.

European Clocks and Watches
BEESON, C. F. C. *English Church Clocks, 1280–1850.* London: Antiquarian Horological Society, 1971.
EDEY, WINTHROP. *French Clocks.* New York: Walker and Co., 1967.
LLOYD, H. ALAN. *Some Outstanding Clocks Over Seven Hundred Years, 1250–1950.* New York: Arco Publishing Co., 1962.
LOOMES, BRIAN. *The White Dial Clock.* New York: Drake Publishers, 1975.

Some Public Collections of Clocks and Watches

Index

Acknowledgments

This book was realized through the efforts of many people, only one of whom was the author. In preparing the content, I was greatly aided by the thoughtful criticisms and helpful suggestions of Chris H. Bailey, Edward F. LaFond, Jr., and Clare Vincent, each of whom read the manuscript and contributed much to its improvement. (I still claim full responsibility for any remaining inadequacies or inaccuracies, however.) For assistance received in the course of assembling the illustrative material, I am indebted to the private collectors and museum staff members who made their treasures available to me. I especially thank Chris Bailey, in this case in his capacity as Director-Curator of the American Clock and Watch Museum, and Carlene Stephens of the Smithsonian Institution's National Museum of History and Technology for their cooperation in arranging special photography. For help with various other aspects of the project, I am grateful to Joseph Del Valle, Brenda Gilchrist, Joan Hoffman, Lisa Little and Joyce O'Connor, each of whom has proved to be a congenial colleague. Finally, to whomever these words are due, I say wholeheartedly, "Thank you for letting me do this book."   DOUGLAS H. SHAFFER

Cooper-Hewitt staff members have been responsible for the following contributions to the series: concept, Lisa Taylor; administration, Christian Rohlfing, David McFadden and Kurt Struver; coordination, Pamela Theodoredis. In addition, valuable help has been provided by S. Dillon Ripley, Joseph Bonsignore, Susan Hamilton and Robert W. Mason of the Smithsonian Institution, as well as by the late Warren Lynch, Gloria Norris and Edward E. Fitzgerald of Book-of-the-Month Club, Inc.

Credits